THE LORD OF ALL GOOD LIFE

A STUDY OF THE GREATNESS OF JESUS
AND THE WEAKNESS OF HIS CHURCH

BY
DONALD HANKEY
AUTHOR OF "A STUDENT IN ARMS"

FOURTH IMPRESSION

LONGMANS, GREEN AND CO.
39 PATERNOSTER ROW, LONDON
FOURTH AVENUE AND 30TH STREET, NEW YORK
BOMBAY, CALCUTTA, AND MADRAS
1917

All rights reserved

BIBLIOGRAPHICAL NOTE

First Edition, October 1914.
New Impressions, February 1917,
April 1917, *July* 1917.

DEDICATED TO
THE LAITY OF THE CHURCH
OF ENGLAND

Digitized for Microsoft Corporation
by the Internet Archive in 2007
From University of California Libraries.
May be used for non-commercial, personal, research,
or educational purposes, or any fair use.
May not be indexed in a commercial service

FOREWORD

THIS is the book of a nobody—of the obscurest of mere laymen. It has no weight of scholastic or ecclesiastical fame behind it. Yet such as it is, it is honest. It is the attempt of a layman—perhaps of a heretic—to think clearly. He is not concerned to " temper the wind (of criticism) to the shorn lamb," nor anxious to " reassure " anyone. He is not a Superior Person, and does not itch to " enlighten " the old-fashioned with " the new knowledge." This book claims neither to be " a contribution to scholarship," nor " apologetic." The writer has tried to set down what he believes a great many people think—people who are not very much enamoured of ecclesiastical controversy, or of patristic theology, or of sung matins at eleven, nor yet, perhaps, of high mass at twelve, who put but little confidence in bishops or university professors, and have little respect for dogmas which seem to be at variance with facts as far as they know them ; and yet feel that in Jesus Christ and in His Church, and at the quiet service on a Sunday morning early, there is power and love and life of which they are in sore need.

If it helps anyone to think their thoughts more articulately; if it gives to anyone the expression, however inadequate, of something that they too

FOREWORD

have known, but have not had time or knowledge to work out, it will have done its work.

To the laity of the Church of England, to all who in shops and factories and barrack-rooms and messes and colleges and hospitals and ships, and wherever else men are gathered together, are trying to fight the battle of Christ with the poorest of equipment, this book is dedicated in loving fellowship.

7TH BATTALION RIFLE BRIGADE,
    OUDENARDE BARRACKS,
        ALDERSHOT.

October, 1914.

CONTENTS

PART I

JESUS OF NAZARETH: HIS LIFE AND WORK.

Chapter		Page
I	The Birth of the Lord Jesus and His Growth	15
II	The Coming of the Kingdom	18
III	The Call of Jesus to be the Christ	21
IV	How the Lord Jesus was Tempted	23
V	How the Lord Jesus began His Work	28
VI	The Teaching of Jesus About the Kingdom	32
VII	The Teaching of Jesus About the Kingdom (*continued*)	44
VIII	How the Pharisees Received the Teaching of Jesus	53
IX	How the Common People Received the Message of the Kingdom	63

CONTENTS

Chapter		Page
X	The Disciples	69
XI	Jerusalem	75
XII	The Death of Jesus	86
XIII	What Happened Afterwards	91

PART II

THE CHURCH: ITS IDEAL, ITS FAILURE, AND ITS FUTURE.

Chapter		Page
I	Definition of the Church	97
II	Protestantism	105
III	Catholicism	111
IV	Protestant Catholicism	118
V	Catholic Worship	122
VI	Catholic Teaching	132
VII	Catholic Warfare	144
VIII	Catholic Warfare (*continued*)	150
IX	The Way of Salvation	158
X	Conclusion	161

CONTENTS

APPENDICES

		PAGE
I	THE VIRGIN BIRTH AND THE EMPTY TOMB	163
II	THE MIRACLES OF JESUS	165
III	THE RELATIVE VALUE OF THE GOSPELS	169

PART I

JESUS OF NAZARETH : HIS LIFE AND WORK

CHAPTER I

THE BIRTH OF THE LORD JESUS AND HIS GROWTH

THE Lord Jesus was once a small baby. Like other babies, He could not talk, or reason, or even walk. As a baby, He had neither knowledge nor power. He was ignorant of history, of nature, and of theology. He was ignorant of Himself.

He looked around Him and touched things. He looked into His mother's eyes and learnt to love. He drew nourishment from her breast. His mind began to grow, feeding on the objects with which His senses brought Him into contact. He learnt to talk, to ask questions, to think, to connect things in His mind, and to differentiate between them. He was told about God.

Later on He was sent to the Synagogue, and was taught the law of Moses, the history of His nation, the sermons of the prophets, and the songs of the psalmists. All these things He pondered over, and His mind went on growing.

Meanwhile He lived at home, loving and obeying His mother, playing with the other village boys, learning to be a carpenter. We have no description of Him at this time; but from what He afterwards was we can tell to some extent what He must have been. The child is father to the man. The thing that distinguished Him from the other village boys was the thing that all through His life set Him apart. It was His love for God. To Him God seemed so real, so near. He thought about Him constantly. Everything reminded Him of God—the flowers, the seed growing up in the fields, the vines bringing forth their fruit, the love of home. He thought about God as His Father—perhaps He was told that Joseph was not His father—and it seemed the most important thing in life to "be about His Father's business." It was not difficult to Him to be good. The greatness and goodness of God so filled His mind with happiness that it made Him naturally humble, loving, and self-forgetful.

Yet other people seemed to find it so hard to be good. They found it so hard to feel the reality of God. They were continually made miserable by fits of anger, fancied slights, disappointed hopes. It was gradually borne in on Jesus that in this respect He was different to other men. This gave Him a sense of destiny. It did not make Him proud, but rather humble and tender—humble because God had singled Him out for this great happiness, and tender because other people had not received the same gift as He.

No doubt He could be terribly angry at a mean, cowardly, or brutal action; but His was white anger, not red. His anger was against the deed, and not against the doer, and it was never on His own account.

So He grew up, in favour with God and man, a common village boy, and yet a boy apart; loved, and yet a little feared too, because He was not quite understood. On the whole, probably the people of Nazareth were rather relieved than otherwise when He and His mother moved to Capernaum, leaving only His married sisters behind at Nazareth.

THE BIRTH OF JESUS AND HIS GROWTH

Capernaum was a fishing town on the shore of the Sea of Galilee. Jesus soon made friends there, especially among the fishermen. One of these was named Simon, who, though he was older than Jesus, loved Him with a love that he simply could not express.

Still no sign came to Jesus of the work that He was to do, and He went on with His ordinary work as a carpenter, watching and praying so as to be ready when His call should come.

CHAPTER II

THE COMING OF THE KINGDOM

AT that time all good Jews were looking forward to the coming of the kingdom of God. It might be long in coming, but they were certain that sooner or later it would arrive; and it was this certainty that enabled them to go on being faithful to their religion.

The position of the Jews was this:

1. They believed that they alone of all the nations on the earth worshipped the true God.

2. For centuries they had been oppressed and persecuted by heathen nations.

Over and over again they had been conquered, their holy temple spoiled, their treasures taken from them. Persians, Greeks, Egyptians, Syrians had been their masters, and their God had been openly defied and derided by the worshippers of idols. Only once had He delivered them, and that was about 150 years ago, when Antiochus Epiphanes, king of Syria, had tried to extirpate their religion. Then, indeed, God had raised up deliverers in the persons of the Maccabean brothers, and their phenomenal success had kindled the hope that the kingdom of God was not far distant. But now they were a subject nation again, with a Roman governor in Jerusalem.

Obviously, this sort of thing could not go on for ever. In the end God must vindicate His honour,

THE COMING OF THE KINGDOM

reward the Jews for their fidelity, and punish the heathen for their blasphemies. Sooner or later the kingdom of God must come, when His sovereignty would be established through all the world. And in that kingdom the faithful Jews should receive great honour and comfort, but the apostates and blasphemers should suffer terrible things.

The expectation of the kingdom was the logical result of faith in the God of Israel. It was the one thing that made that faith possible. Also it had been foretold by the prophets.

It was to the writings of the prophets that the pious Jews turned when they wanted to find out what sort of a kingdom it would be, and what would be the manner of its coming. This study of the prophets seems to have resulted in the expectation that first of all Elijah would return to earth, and warn men to prepare. Then a descendant of King David would arise, to be known as the Christ (anointed one) or Messiah. He would begin the discomfiture of the heathen. Finally, there would be signs in the heaven and on the earth, the heathen and the apostates be destroyed by a series of natural catastrophes, and the faithful dead rise from their graves to share in the joy of the kingdom.

Probably, opinions varied a good deal as to the exact manner in which the kingdom would come. Some seem to have thought that it would be preceded by a great war in which the Jews would conquer the world. Others, perhaps, expected God Himself to descend from Heaven. At the time of the last Jewish revolt in A.D. 132, a man called Bar Cochbar was thought by many to be the Messiah, and his followers expected God to intervene just when things were at their worst. But whatever differences of opinion there may have been, it is certain that all good Jews expected that sooner or later, by force of arms or natural catastrophe, the kingdom of God would come, and that its coming was to be the crowning event of all the history of the past.

Jesus also looked for the coming of the kingdom, though, as He had different ideas about God to those of other men, His expectation of the kingdom was probably also unique in many features.

Suddenly a prophet arose, John the Baptist. He appeared on the banks of the Jordan with the startling message that the kingdom was close at hand, and that he was sent to prepare men for it.

CHAPTER III

THE CALL OF JESUS TO BE THE CHRIST

JOHN the Baptist proclaimed the coming of a kingdom which should be preceded by judgment. One was to come after him, whose shoe he was not worthy to loose, whose task it would be to purge the nation of all apostates and hypocrites, and to gather together all true Israelites to share in the glories of the kingdom. His own work was simply to warn men to repent of their sins, so that when the Christ should come they would be included with the faithful, and not cast out with the faithless. As a sign of repentance on their part, and as a symbol of the cleansing which was necessary before they would be fit to receive the kingdom, John baptized his disciples in the river Jordan.

There was tremendous excitement at John's preaching. He seemed like one of the old prophets come to life. The absence of any personal claim, and the insistence on the necessity of moral reformation, stamped him as one of their line. Crowds went to hear him, and to be baptized by him.

Among others, Jesus and some of His friends went. Jesus had long felt that till people could know and love God, and give up their sins, there could be no kingdom of God on earth. He had long realized that though there were plenty of people who professed to be religious, and went regularly to the synagogue on the sabbath, and to Jerusalem for the feasts, who hated the heathen and Samaritans as the enemies of God, and loathed the apostate Jews who disregarded the law; yet there were hardly any who really knew God, or lived holy lives. Therefore, He, too, was attracted by John, who was preaching what He knew to be true—that the way to prepare for the kingdom was to repent and wash one's soul clean.

Jesus wanted to be at one with all these people who were trying to purify themselves against the coming of the kingdom; so He too went to the banks of the Jordan, and asked John for baptism. But when John fixed his piercing eyes on Jesus, as though to make sure that His repentance was genuine, he saw a face on which there was no trace of sin, the face of One who all His life had walked with God, and was full of grace and truth. "It is I that need to be baptized by Thee," John protested.

Jesus, however, insisted. He wanted to fulfil all righteousness; to be one with His brother men in every effort they made to prepare for the kingdom. Then a wonderful thing happened, for as Jesus came up out of the water He saw the heavens opened, and the Spirit as a dove descending upon Him; while a voice said to Him, "Thou art my beloved Son, in Thee I am well pleased."

NOTE

This is St. Mark's account of the baptism of Jesus. It is worth noticing that according to St. John (John i. 32 to 34) John the Baptist also saw the Spirit descend upon Him.

CHAPTER IV

How the Lord Jesus was Tempted

At His baptism, Jesus underwent a wonderful and, in some ways, a terrifying experience. As when a man is suddenly " converted " he sees everything in a new light, and understands in a moment what has hitherto been perplexing and mysterious, so it was with Jesus. That sense of destiny, that difference between Himself and other men which had hitherto been an unexplained mystery, were suddenly explained. He was good because He was God's Son, and in order that He might impart to other men the love and knowledge of His Father which He alone possessed. He was the Christ, the destined reconciler of men with God, the anointed founder of God's kingdom on earth. Moreover, He felt that at the moment of His baptism He had been given the power to accomplish His work. He felt that the Holy Spirit of God had descended upon Him, and anointed Him with power and wisdom and love, that He might worthily obey His call.

He did not hesitate, He trusted the call, and immediately withdrew to the desert to think out His plans in the presence of God alone. Forty days He spent in the desert, fasting, praying, trying to foresee the dangers He would have to meet, and to understand how best to use the powers that God had given Him for the task that God had set Him.

It was during those forty days that He faced the temptation which comes to all prophets, the temptation to set a limit on His reliance on God, and to rely instead on His own personal gifts. This temptation came to Him in three forms.

To begin with, was He sure in His own mind that He was the Son of God ? Now that all the excitement was over, was He sure that He had not deceived Himself ? After all, His call had been subjective. Perhaps he had been abnormally worked up. Ought He not to be sure before He made this assumption—an assumption which amounted to blasphemy if it was not true ? Besides, if it were untrue He would fail miserably. What assurance had He that if He gave up His ordinary work He would even be able to live ?

So the temptation took form. "If thou art Son of God," whispered the tempter, "command that these stones be made bread."

Then He would know whether God had called Him or not. Having an objective sign to go on, He would know that God would give Him everything else needful for the founder of the kingdom.

The Lord Jesus set aside the temptation. He trusted God. Moreover, His call, and the revelation of His office in the world, had not destroyed His humility. It was not His own glory that He was going to seek in the founding of the kingdom. It was not in blasphemous self-assertion that He was going to set about His work ; but in humility, and if God willed, in hunger and poverty. He was the Son of God. He believed it. But all that that meant was that with a son's obedience, and with a son's confidence, He would be about His Father's business. He would trust God in the great matter of His call,

HOW THE LORD JESUS WAS TEMPTED

and in the smaller matter of the means. The result would be His sign.

"Man does not live by bread alone, but by every word that proceedeth out of the mouth of God." "My meat is to do the will of Him that sent me."

If every word that God spoke was going to be doubted and tested by a sign, what meaning was there in faith ?

But, even granting that He was right not to demand a sign for Himself, ought He not to ask one for the sake of the people ? How could He ask the Jews to believe that a poor carpenter was the Christ ?

He imagined Himself standing on a pinnacle of the temple, looking down upon a sea of upturned faces—devout Jews gathered in the court below for some great feast. The voice of the tempter whispers, " If thou be Son of God, cast thyself down ; for it is written, He shall give His angels charge concerning thee, and on their hands shall they bear thee up, lest haply thou dash thy foot against a stone."

He could picture the result. There would be a mighty shout, " A sign ! A sign from heaven ! The Christ is come to His people ! Jesus is the Christ ! " There could be no doubt. The news would fly from village to village. The people would flock to Him. The kingdom would be half won already. Moreover, where would be the harm ? He would simply have used His power for the very purpose for which it was given—for the founding of the kingdom.

"Thou shalt not tempt the Lord thy God."

If Jesus was the Christ there was no need for such a sign. It could safely be left to God to demonstrate the fact in His own time and in His own way. Moreover, what sort of faith was it that would be kindled by such a sign, or that needed such a sign to kindle it ? Not the faith that trusts in bad times as in good, in the dark as in the light. Not the loving faith that makes the sinner turn from his sin. Not a faith that would have any merit or value, or that would prepare men for the kingdom of God, or make them fit to enter it.

And yet what possibilities there were in the faith that such a sign would evoke ! With the undoubting allegiance of the troops that had served the Maccabees so well; with the help of Him whom the sun and the storm and all the forces of nature obey, where would be the power of Herod or Pilate, or of Cæsar himself ?

After all, some of the prophets had expected the kingdom to come in this way, and was there not a wealth of vengeance due to the heathen for their treatment of God's people ?

Jesus imagined Himself upon a high mountain, with all the countries of the world stretched out before Him. All these might be His if . . . if He worshipped the Spirit of evil.

What sort of kingdom was to be won with the Devil's weapons ? Not a kingdom of God. Not a kingdom of love. No, but a very Devil's kingdom. A kingdom of fear and cruelty, of the lust and pride of the victors, and the servile, grudging obedience of the vanquished.

" Thou shalt worship the Lord thy God, and Him only shalt thou serve."

There was no short cut to the kingdom. It could only be won by love that knew no limit. Only by setting out on His mission in poverty and humility and boundless faith could the Christ persuade men that the unseen was more real than the seen, the spirit than the flesh ; that love was more divine than power, and more to be coveted than riches ; that the kingdom of God was a kingdom of love and peace; that servants were its princes, and humility its glory; that its foes were not heathen and Samaritans, but lust, oppression, violence, hypocrisy, meanness, and cowardice. And until men realized this, how could the kingdom come?

Jesus had resolved not to assert Himself; not to work miracles, either to supply His own necessity or to convince the sceptical; and not to attempt to found the kingdom of God by force of arms. He was going to be a prophet and a teacher, and to trust to God to bring in the kingdom, and to vindicate His Son.

"Angels came and ministered to Him."

CHAPTER V

How the Lord Jesus began His Work

The Lord Jesus had received His call, He had faced the difficulties which confronted Him, made His plans, counted the cost, and now it was time for Him to begin His real work. He therefore went back to Capernaum to lay the foundations of the kingdom.

Full of zeal for the kingdom, and, like a good workman, forgetting Himself in His enthusiasm for the work, He said nothing about His being the Christ, but at first only repeated the message of John—"Repent, for the kingdom of heaven is at hand." His plan was to teach first the nature of the kingdom, and to leave people to deduce for themselves who was the Christ.

His first action was to call upon some of His friends to follow Him, so that to them at least He might make certain of imparting the truth that was in Him. As He passed along the shore of the lake He summoned Simon and Andrew, James and John, saying, "Come ye after me, and I will make you to become fishers of men." And immediately they left their nets and followed Him.

Then, on the very next Sabbath, when the people were assembled at the synagogue to hear the reading of the law and the prophets, He began His work of teaching.

But at the outset there was a difficulty, for some half-witted fellow, in whom the people of those days

HOW JESUS BEGAN HIS WORK

thought there was a devil, began to cry out with a loud voice, " What have we to do with thee, thou Jesus of Nazareth ? Art thou come to destroy us ? I know thee who thou art, the holy one of God."[1]

This was the last thing that Jesus wanted to happen. It drew attention to His person at the expense of His message, and so reversed the order in which He wanted the understanding of the kingdom to come. He looked at the man, and felt that He could cure him; so, partly out of pity, and partly to stop his crying out, he rebuked him, and said, " Hold thy peace, and come out of him." And the man uttered a loud cry, underwent a sort of convulsion, and returned to his right mind.

This cure caused something of a sensation, and Jesus' manner of teaching proved equally astonishing; for whereas the scribes were accustomed merely to comment on scripture, and to use for the most part second-hand comments, Jesus spoke His own opinion,

---

[1] It was the cry of a madman, a man who had no self-control; who arrived at conclusions, not by reasoning, but by a sort of instinct, and must needs blurt out whatever came into his head. The instinct of a sane man is disciplined by his reason, and its articulation is controlled. When we receive an impression, it is immediately seized upon by our mind, compared with our previous impressions, qualified by the prejudices and preconceived ideas that we have accumulated; and by the time that it has reached articulation in thought or speech the original impression is hardly recognizable. But this poor fellow's mind was unhinged, and the impression that Jesus made on him got translated into words straight away, mixed up with his *idée fixe* that he was possessed by a devil, but otherwise unedited by the mind. And so the truth was out before anyone could stop it.

There is no reason to doubt that Jesus Himself shared the general idea that the man was possessed by a devil. If the diagnosis of mental disease is a matter for scientific investigation, Jesus doubtless shared the views of His contemporaries. If it is to be decided by the religious sense, Jesus is more likely to have been right than we are. Anyhow, the faith that the personality of Jesus inspired focussed the man's mind, and enabled his reason to assert its power of control.

on its own authority. After the meeting was over, people turned to each other and said, " With what authority he teacheth ! He is not like the scribes. And with what authority he commandeth the unclean spirits, and they obey him."

From the very start it was the personality of Jesus that attracted attention. His assurance in teaching, the consistency between His teaching and His life, the correspondence between His teaching and the conscience of His hearers, His humility and poverty, and His marvellous power of healing the sick and the mad, inevitably set people asking, " Who is he ? Whence hath he this wisdom and power ? Is he not the carpenter ? " And so from the first His faith was justified. There was no need of a sign to point Him out. Simply by what it was, His personality challenged imperiously either passionate devotion or venomous fear.

The immediate effect of the morning's work was to draw attention to Jesus. Crowds came to Him, though probably more came to be healed or to see others healed than came to hear Him preach. That very evening they brought all the sick people of the little town to Him, and out of sheer pity He could not refuse to employ the power to heal that had been given Him by the great Giver of all life.

At last the day came to an end, and the tired people went home to bed. But when Simon and the other disciples looked for Jesus the next day, they found that very early in the morning He had gone off to a desert place to be alone with God, and to pray. They found Him, and said, " All are seeking thee." Jesus answered, " Let us go elsewhere into the next towns, that I may preach there also ; for to this end came I forth."

The next cure that is recorded by St. Mark was that of a leper, and it is significant that Jesus strictly charged him to say nothing to any man. He had come to the conclusion that though He could not refuse to do good, and to use His good gift of healing, He must do all He could to keep that side of His work in the background, so that it should not interfere with the preaching of the kingdom.

Unfortunately, the leper published the matter everywhere, so that Jesus could not enter a village openly without being besieged by sick people, and people wanting to see cures. He had to remain in desert places, to which crowds came to hear Him.

For a long time after this, Jesus just travelled about Galilee, teaching and healing. One of His favourite ways of avoiding a crush was to enter a fishing boat, and, putting off a little from the shore, teach from there. At this period He was immensely popular, and crowds followed Him about.

CHAPTER VI

THE TEACHING OF JESUS ABOUT THE KINGDOM

Why Jesus was the Christ.

Many prophets, of whom the last was John the Baptist, had foretold the coming of the kingdom, yet no one had suspected them of being the Christ. Jesus also foretold the coming of the kingdom, but in such a manner that, without any announcement on His part, His disciples came to the conclusion that He was the Christ, and his enemies accused Him of claiming that title. The reason was that whereas the prophets had referred to the kingdom as a goal in the remote future to which they looked forward, Jesus spoke of it as something that was at once present and future; which could be entered by the individual now; and which would become the inheritance of all good people, alive and dead, in the future. Jesus spoke not as one that saw the kingdom afar off; but as one who already possessed it, and belonged to it. He spoke as the King's Son. This was the note of originality in His teaching.

The New Birth: or how to enter the kingdom.

To know and to feel the reality of God was, in the eyes of Jesus, to have entered into possession of the kingdom. The heart where God was recognized as sole ruler was already a part of the kingdom, and there the peace of the kingdom was already enjoyed.

The ordinary man has what seemed to Jesus a very distorted sense of perspective. He sees the material things which perish so very big, that he can't see God at all. But once a man has got a true sense of perspective he will realize that, if God matters at all, He matters so much that nothing else matters in the least by comparison with Him. The man who thinks that money, or position, or popularity, or life itself is of great importance, has got his horizon so blocked up that he can't see God. Before he can see God he has got to clear away all his prejudices and preconceived ideas, cherished ambitions, and axiomatic principles, which have been based on a faulty view of life—one which has left out and ignored the ruling factor, even God. He has got to begin all over again, and start to revise all his ideas as to the relative importance of things. He has got to become simple and humble and unprejudiced, like a little child. He has got to be born again into a new life in which all that has hitherto seemed big and important is seen to be small and insignificant; while the one outstanding feature, which gives their meaning to all the others, is God. And the faculties in himself which have hitherto seemed most of doubtful value, will appear the only ones which have any value at all. They are the faculties which link him to God—love, faith, humility, and purity. The man who has undergone this transformation is a new man; he has been born again. He has entered the kingdom of heaven, and possesses its peace.

But it is not easy to be born again. Before the rich man can enter the kingdom he must realize that his wealth is so comparatively unimportant that he is ready to give it all away rather than allow it to obscure his vision of God, and hinder him from entering the kingdom. The man of good social position must be prepared to become the servant of the poorest and meanest. The passionate man must be ready to cut off his hand, pluck out his eye, or even become a eunuch rather than lose the kingdom for the sake of indulging his passions. The Jew must be prepared to fraternize with the Samaritan, and the Pharisee with the publican, and on equal terms; admitting the possibility that they whom before he despised and abhorred are very likely better and nearer to God's ideal than himself. All must be ready to give up friends, home, wealth, position, life itself, rather than miss entering the kingdom of heaven.

The kingdom is like a pearl of great price, or a treasure hid in a field, for which, when he has once understood its value, a man will gladly barter all that he possesses.

The New Life.

But where so many people make a mistake is that they imagine that there is some virtue inherent in giving up. This is a most disastrous fallacy, and it is this which has made Christianity stink among wholesome-minded people. Giving up for its own sake is a narrowing proceeding ; whereas the giving up recommended by Jesus Christ had for its object a fuller, freer, less restricted life. The lesser good is only to be given up when it blocks the way for the greater. The wealth of this world is only to be given up to secure the riches of eternity. A man is only to leave home, and incur the loss of his former friends and associates in order that he may find a new Father in God, and new brothers and sisters and mothers in everyone that is trying to obey God's will. There is no virtue in self-mutilation, for a man should love God with every faculty that he possesses; it is only when the perverted activities of certain members are poisoning the whole body, and preventing the soul from living the new life of the kingdom, that those members must be sacrificed.

The pain and travail of the new birth are justified by the glorious beauty and fulness and freedom of the new life. The new life is more harmonious than the old, because it is based on a true sense of proportion; it is fuller than the old because the best part of a man—his spirit, which has hitherto been stifled, is now made articulate and brought into conscious relations with the source of all good life—God. The new man is guided by new motives, and has a new goal in view. He no longer uses base means to attain worthless ends; but uses all the best faculties that he possesses in trying to make God's kingdom realized, His will obeyed, His name hallowed on earth as it is in heaven; and in doing so is trying to bring out all the beauty and goodness and wholesomeness of life, and to destroy all that tends to mar and to restrict life.

Characteristics of the New Life.

We shall best understand this by studying some of the chief characteristics of the new life. The vision of God means faith in Him and love for Him, humility and the desire for purity in oneself, and love for one's fellow men. And these involve freedom and courage and peace and power.

FAITH

Faith is the power to see God. It is the vision of the unseen. It is the eye that is able to penetrate below the material surface and see the underlying Spirit of God. It is faith that gives a man the right sense of proportion, the new perspective, which results in the new life. It was faith which Jesus possessed in the supreme degree, and which was His chief gift to men.

To begin with, fear is impossible to the man who has faith, who has understood the reality of the love of God.

A man cannot fear physical danger if he really has faith; for God is the source of all good life, and the Lord of death.

When the disciples of Jesus were in danger of shipwreck, and awoke Him up in alarm for their safety, He said, " What, have ye not yet faith ? " If they had had faith they would not have worried. They would have done all they could calmly and bravely, knowing that if after that they perished it was a sign that their work in the world was finished, and that God was calling them to work elsewhere. Fear and worry are useless and senseless, if only we could realize it. They accomplish nothing, and rather hinder.

Similarly, it is unthinkable that the man who has faith should fear men. At the worst, men can only kill the body, and what does the death of the body matter if one believes in the God of the spirit ? If God matters, men do not matter. What they say and think and threaten does not count. The man of faith is free to make right decisions without fear or favour.

Nor must the man of faith be a prey to worldly anxieties. If God clothes the flowers and feeds the sparrows, He will feed His human children. To do one's best in faith is better than any amount of worry. After all, most worry comes from unwillingness to accept a conventionally lower standard of life than what we are accustomed to. Yet the man who has faith and love can be as happy in a workhouse as anywhere else. He has treasure that no one can take from him—the kingdom of God within. Jesus was often hungry and homeless, but it did not worry Him, for His meat was to do His Father's will.

The man who has faith is also free from the tyranny of passion and inherent weakness. It is true that men are normally slaves of their hereditary tendencies as modified by the circumstances of their education and surroundings. A man is the meeting-place of forces over which he has little control, and they will mould his life unless some stronger force is introduced to counteract them. But if a man has been born again and has the eye of faith, a new factor, a dominating factor has entered the environment of which he is conscious ; and it is the thought of God which will over-ride and nullify all contrary influences, even those of heredity and habit.

Finally, the man who has faith will not be subject to false ambitions. Having once seen the true good, he will see at a glance the spuriousness of the imitation.

Thus in the kingdom of God there are no physical or moral cowards, no slaves of passion, weakness, or false ambition. All are fearless and altogether free; and in the records of the life of Jesus Christ will be found ample indications that He Himself possessed the fearlessness and freedom of faith which He preached. There is no sign that He was ever influenced by the fear of men or of physical danger, that He was ever anxious, or that He was ever swayed by passion or false ambition.

LOVE FOR GOD

For Jesus, to know God was to love Him. His Father in Heaven was the giver of all life, the author of all beauty in nature, the source of all goodness in man. And to love is to want to give.

But what can a man give to God, when all good things are given by Him?

Thanks to our ignorance, and to the pain and doubt and evil in the world, we can give Him trust and obedience and honour and worship which have some value in His sight. If we saw and knew everything, our love would have no value; it would have no power of giving.

Jesus did not know or see except through faith. His call was "subjective"; to Him, too, came the temptation to doubt. His death was the offering of the supreme gift of a love which was born of faith, and which was of value simply for that reason.

HUMILITY

The man who sees God very big, naturally sees himself very small. The centre of his universe is shifted from himself to God. It will no longer seem of great importance whether he himself is honoured or slighted by men, as long as he is loved by God. He will no longer be sensitive to snubs, insults, or the humiliation of failure. He will no longer push himself forward, and seek "the most honourable seat at the feast." In humility he will find freedom from much that destroys the peace and happiness of most men.

He will not set much store by the things that distinguish him from his neighbours. He will not let the accidents of birth, position, education, etc., shut him up in a narrow groove, and cut him off from his fellow-men. He will not be self-righteous or smug. Compared with the difference between himself and God, the degree of wealth, honour, wisdom, refinement, and even goodness which separates him from other men, will almost disappear. Before the throne of God all men are poor, ignorant, coarse, and evil, and all are able to become rich, wise, holy, and good, for all are able to become children of God, and heirs of His kingdom.

In other words the man of faith will be neither a prig nor a snob, for there are none in the kingdom of heaven. And he will find that the world for him has become much bigger. Even if he is disowned by the little coterie in which he was born, he will have become a citizen of the great world, an inheritor of the earth in the fullest sense.

It was this feature of Christ's teaching and character that gave most offence to the respectable people of Palestine. He would not honour the Pharisee rather than the publican, the sinner, and the harlot. He was friends with them all. He shamed the faults of all, and tried to bring out the inherent goodness in them all. All were needed for the kingdom ; all were beloved of God ; all needed the new birth, and were capable of the new life. And it is this feature of Christ's teaching and character which the church has most conspicuously failed to appropriate. Religion has an almost inevitable tendency towards smugness and snobbishness. Often and often the churches have been more akin to the Pharisees than to their alleged Master in this matter, and have consequently failed miserably to increase the kingdom.

PURITY

Contact with God necessitates purity. It is only the pure that see God. But purity is not the same as conventional morality, it is a quality of the heart. It is the love of clean, vigorous, healthy life, and the hatred of all that is destructive of health and sanity, all that is corrupt and filthy. It is an essential characteristic of the love of God simply because God is the Source of life.

As a matter of fact, the crimes that society punishes most heavily are not always the worst crimes against God. It is possible to imagine even a murder inspired by an abhorrence of the human reptile. It is very easy to imagine—in fact there is no need for imagination—there are many cases where theft of a straightforward kind should trouble the conscience of society more than that of the thief. The worst crimes against God are the crimes that degrade the man who commits them—cringing, meanness, cowardice, indolence, lying, treachery, back-biting, seduction, lust, and the like. These pollute the heart of a man, and cut him off from the Source of all good life.

Here again Jesus gives us the perfect example of one who loathed all kinds of filth and cant and meanness, and yet whose loathing was more than the mere shrinking of the sensitive and æsthetic soul. His aim was always to remove the evil, and he did not shrink from contact with any foul or degraded thing if by contact He could heal and restore to health. He touched the leper. He allowed the harlot to wash His feet with her tears. He suffered the shame and agony and degradation of the Cross that He might rob it of its terror.

The purity of Jesus was not negative but positive. It was the love of wholesome life which continually urged Him to the work of restoration, and to combat the forces of corruption.

THE TEACHING ABOUT THE KINGDOM

THE HOLY ENERGY OF LOVE

Jesus has been called "the pale Galilean," and Christianity has been accused of being negative. It has been said that Jesus taught men to despise the real world and to live in a dream world. The Christian life has been represented as lacking in virility, as consisting in renunciation, and a sort of wallowing in failure and misery. We have already indicated the exactly opposite view. The God of Jesus is not like the supreme being of Brahminism, a being who, as all-inclusive, must be without external environment, and therefore devoid of external activity. The God of Jesus is the eternal Father, the eternal Giver of life, whose nature is to give life and to love. As the shepherd yearns after the lost sheep, so God yearns after the sinner. As a father welcomes the returning prodigal, so God welcomes the repentant sinner. As a woman rejoices over the finding of a lost coin, so there is joy in heaven over the soul that has turned to its God. So, too, the man who has had the vision of God will go back to his daily life with new energy and zest, for he will have burning in him the fire of love.

Life, according to Jesus, is like when a man goes on a journey, and leaves his servants in charge of his goods. One gets five talents, another ten. Their duty is to use these talents in their master's service with as much zeal and energy as possible, so that when he returns they may be fit to receive greater responsibilities still—five cities, ten cities. The unforgivable fault is to waste opportunities, to be indolent.

The two great commandments, according to Jesus, are to love God with all one's heart and soul and mind and strength, and one's neighbour as oneself. Both are positive commandments. To love God properly demands the exercise of every faculty that we possess —heart, soul, mind, strength. To love one's neighbour as oneself means to do to all men what one would they should do to oneself. It is illustrated in the gospel story by the parable of the good Samaritan, showing that what is required is active and practical charity.

One has only to look at the life of Jesus to see what an active thing the love that He preached is. He was continually showing up hypocrisy and cant, exposing men's lack of charity, and trying to galvanize them into putting their beliefs into active commission. He was continually using His power to heal both mind and body. To fight all the forces which stunt and corrupt and limit life; to break down all the conventions and traditions and prejudices which paralyse men's freedom to live and love; and so to make the world more and more a kingdom of the life-giving and loving God, this was the task of Jesus and His disciples. And the fire of inspiration which flamed up in words and deeds of power came from their faith —their vision of God.

The kingdom of God is a vitalizing force, making the dead live, the blind see, the deaf hear, the sick whole, and the prisoner free. It is like leaven, a little of which leavens a whole lump. It is like salt, penetrating and giving flavour to life. It is like light, set on a stand so as to make life clear.

POWER

The freedom and courage, the calm and inward peace, the humility and purity, the energy of love, the contact with the Source of all clean wholesome life—these things make the man who is really born again into the kingdom of God a power for good unequalled in life. The whole edifice of faith rests on a gigantic assumption—the assumption that the dreams of the soul are truer than the sight of the eyes; that the subjective is more real than the objective. Jesus made this assumption. It was born in Him to make it. The truth of it is proved by the fact that this view of life produced a character more noble, more admirable, more potent to inspire love and devotion, more free, more harmonious, more complete than any other in the history of the world. It is also proved if it is true that He rose from the dead, and is alive for evermore; and if in the lives of those who try to follow Him and to pray to Him there is any sign of approach to the high ideal that He both preached and exemplified.

Because of what He was, and what He taught, and what He is, Jesus holds the place in history and in the hearts of men that is above every place; and though the centuries pass, and other teachers are relegated to their place in the tale of "yesterday's sev'n thousand years," Jesus remains for ever the living Lord of all good life.

CHAPTER VII

THE TEACHING OF JESUS ABOUT THE KINGDOM
(*continued*)

The law of the kingdom.

For the Jews, sin was defined by the law of Moses, which is founded on the ten commandments. For the Jews, the law was the revelation of God's will; and so to break the law was to be ungodly. Jesus, however, saw in the law no more than a first clue. The fullest revelation of God He found in His own best self, in His conscience, and in His love. The law gave the general direction; but there came a time when a man must leave the first guide behind, and trust the conscience which the law had first instructed. Jesus gave no new law. He felt no need of a law Himself, for He had the abiding sense of knowing God, which solved all questions as they arose. It was this "law of God in the heart" that He tried to transfer to His disciples. And as a matter of fact the conscience of Jesus has taken the place of the law for His disciples. It was so from the first. There arose occasions when people had to choose between the letter of the law and the conscience of Jesus, and in so far as they preferred the latter they became His disciples. It was this setting of Himself above the law that constituted His blasphemy in the eyes of the orthodox Jew, and which was at the bottom of the belief of His disciples that He was the Son of God.

THE TEACHING ABOUT THE KINGDOM 45

The following table is an attempt to show how Jesus, explicitly or implicitly, expanded the law in His teaching. It will give some indication of the ethics of the kingdom.

	The Mosaic Law.	*The Law of the kingdom*
First.	I am the Lord thy God: thou shalt have none other gods but me.	Thou shalt love the Lord thy God with all thy heart and soul and mind and strength.
Second.	Thou shalt not make to thyself any graven image . . . . for I the Lord thy God am a jealous God . . .	No man can serve two masters.
Third	Thou shalt not take the name of the Lord thy God in vain: for the Lord will not hold him guiltless that taketh His name in vain.	Swear not at all. Cast not thy pearls before swine. Be not as the hypocrites. Do not blaspheme against the Holy Spirit.
Fourth.	Remember that thou keep holy the Sabbath day	The Sabbath was made for man, not man for the Sabbath.
Fifth.	Honour thy father and mother	Render unto Cæsar the things that are Cæsar's, and unto God the things that are God's.
Sixth.	Thou shalt do no murder.	Love thine enemies. Pray for them that persecute thee. Forgive

		unto seventy times seven. Do to all as thou wouldest they should do to thee.
Seventh.	Thou shalt not commit adultery.	Blessed are the pure in heart for they shall see God. Whom God hath joined together let not man put asunder. He that looketh upon a woman to lust after her has committed adultery with her already in his heart.
Eighth.	Thou shalt not steal.	Lay not up for yourselves treasure upon the earth, but in heaven, where neither rust nor moth corrupt, nor do thieves break through nor steal. Seek ye first the kingdom, and all things shall be added unto you.
Ninth.	Thou shalt not bear false witness	Judge not, lest ye be judged. First pluck the beam out of thine own eye, and then shalt thou see clearly to remove the mote from thy brother's eye.
Tenth.	Thou shalt not covet	Let him that would be great among you be the servant of all.

THE TEACHING ABOUT THE KINGDOM

Many other sentences will probably occur to the reader which might have been added; but Jesus gave no systematic ethical teaching. It was His aim rather to give general principles which each man should apply for himself, or better still a point of view from which the solution of all problems of conduct should be apparent. He did not abrogate the law, but claimed that He fulfilled it,—that the righteousness which was the spontaneous effect of having entered the kingdom was the end which the law was designed to accomplish.

The standard by which Jesus judged sins.

Although we have already touched on the subject under the heading of purity, it will be as well to repeat that the effect of this substitution of an internal for an external law profoundly affects the judgment of the relative seriousness of sins. The Jews, relying on an external law, took an extremely serious view of external sins. Neglect to perform the specified ablutions, to fast and pray at the proper times, and particular infractions of the moral law were harshly judged. On the other hand, Jesus, being guided by an internal law, always looked behind the external act to the internal state of which it was a symptom. The same contrast is noticeable in their several methods of dealing with sin. The aim of the Jew was to inflict a punishment proportionate to the offence, while that of Jesus was to alter the internal conditions which produced it. For instance, in the case of the woman taken in adultery the Jews wanted to inflict the death penalty, whereas Jesus did not want to inflict any penalty at all. He apparently recognized that this was a case where all the blame could not be justly put on the woman, and by His gentleness He tried to produce the state of sorrow and the longing for a clean life which might enable her to sin no more. This harlot was, in the eyes of Jesus, much less sinful and much less repulsive than her accusers. She had sinned and was sorry, and her internal condition was such as to call for sympathy and pity and comfort rather than harshness. At the moment she was not, in herself, sensual and animal, though at a previous moment she may have been. On the contrary, at the moment she was ashamed, and her best self was uppermost. But her accusers were full of coarse, callous brutality. They were in a loathsome state of soul, from the point of view of God, and until Jesus had given them a glimpse of the fact they were quite unaware of it.

The treatment of sin.

Taking this view of sin—that it was a diseased condition of the soul—Jesus had no use for the clumsy machinery of external punishment. He was rather a physician, and as such His first care was to try to make the patient aware of his diseased state, and desirous of restoration to a healthy life. Without that He could do nothing. The Pharisee who, narrow and ungenerous, was really living a hideous, stunted life, and was utterly deficient in all that Jesus called life, and yet was supremely and unalterably satisfied that he was just as he should be, was a patient for whom Jesus could do nothing. On the other hand, the man or woman who was an open sinner, and who knew his or her failure to live the best and most wholesome sort of life, was often just in the condition on which Jesus could exercise His healing power. To begin with, Jesus Himself gave an example of the highest essential wholesomeness. His presence gave

THE TEACHING ABOUT THE KINGDOM 49

out power and holiness and love and purity, and gave the sick soul an embodiment of what it desired. It did not want the narrow, restricted, ungenerous morality of the Pharisee. The Pharisee was therefore incapable of healing. It did want the free, generous, spiritual vitality of Jesus, and therefore Jesus was able to inspire the desire for definite health which was the first condition of recovery. That much gained, Jesus simply told His patient that he was forgiven, and the patient believed him, and, being forgiven, was immediately put into touch with the power which was able to restore him—God, the giver of life.

Forgiveness of sins.

Never has any doctrine been so misrepresented as this Christian doctrine of the forgiveness of sins. Forgiveness does not in the least imply immediate restoration to perfect spiritual health, nor does it imply the removal of the penalties of sin. The thief who is forgiven will remain branded as a thief. He will have to serve the sentence that society inflicts on him. If he has stolen from a poor man, and has spent the proceeds of his theft, the poor man will continue to suffer loss; and the fact that he has repented—for if he has not, he has not received forgiveness—means that the thief has the additional punishment of a stricken conscience. None of these things are remitted by forgiveness. But what has happened is that the thief has realized what a detestable meanness of soul it was that caused him to steal from a poor man, and has learnt to loathe that meanness; and from the moment that he does so he is able to come into touch with the God who is able to eradicate his essential meanness in such a way that, next time he is destitute, he will starve or go to the workhouse. At all events the element of meanness which made the first theft so repulsive will not recur.

Jesus did not forgive sins. He announced that the process was automatic. As soon as the sinner repented, there was joy in heaven. As soon as the prodigal started to return home, his Father set about killing the fatted calf. It is obviously an advantage to the sinner to know that this is so. Jesus, by virtue of His knowledge of God, proclaimed that it was so; and sinners of all ages who have put the matter to the test, have been convinced that His knowledge was not at fault.

For this work alone He deserves the title that is upon this book. Because He showed the good life in all its power and beauty, and because He was able to bring sinners into touch with the healing love of God, He was and is the Lord of all good life.

Precedence in the kingdom.

Naturally, as the views of Jesus about sin were so unconventional, His views about precedence in the kingdom were equally disquieting to the respectable. The worthy Jews thought that the kingdom was to be the preserve of those who had kept the Jewish law. They, judged by Jewish standards, were the righteous—the people after God's own heart. Jesus, however, judging by character rather than by external conformity, was quite sure that a kingdom full of the Pharisees and their disciples would certainly not be a kingdom of God. In the kingdom which He preached there would only be pure, generous, humble souls, for they alone were really capable of religion. In this world it might be the rich and the prosperous

THE TEACHING ABOUT THE KINGDOM 51

and the pushing and the ostentatiously pious who were accounted great, but in the kingdom of God the order of precedence should be exactly reversed. The first would be last, and the last first. Mourners should be comforted, the poor enriched, the humble exalted, the humblest servant would be the greatest. Sinners and harlots should come in before the Pharisees, and Gentiles before the Jews. Those who had the courage to risk their lives for the gospel's sake should find them, but the cowards who would take no risks would lose theirs.

This was not mere epigram. It was the expression of profound truth. The three loathsome types of people are the snobs, the prigs, and the cowards. The first two classes are hopeless because they will not see how loathsome they are, and have no desire for good life; and the cowards do not love it well enough to take any risks. No one can enter the kingdom unless he has a desire to do so, unless he has some longing for the good clean life that comes from God. And it is often the unhappy who have that longing.

The final realization of the kingdom.

St. Paul was right when he said that if Christ were not risen, we were of all men most miserable. If life is not good, if the stream is polluted at its source, and evil breeds evil as good breeds good all through the ages, then their labour is vain that try to cleanse it. But if life is essentially good, if it flows from the good God, and will be purified in the end in His eternal kingdom from all the impurities that it has picked up; then it is worth while to strive for better life and more life, for we are working in harmony with the course of nature. This is the source of happiness and peace—to work in harmony with the object of creation. If creation has no object, it is much better to be a cynic. Altruism without hope is unscientific folly. Jesus had a hope amounting to certainty that the kingdom of God was going to be realized perfectly in the end. The kingdom is like seed. It grows gradually, imperceptibly ; but it is destined to end by being all-embracing. The time for discrimination is not yet. Till the harvest is ripe the tares and the corn, the chaff and the grain must be allowed to grow together ; but in the end the tares and chaff will be burnt up, and the good grain gathered into barns.

In that day the Christ shall come to His own. Those who have confessed Him before men shall He claim in the presence of His Father. Those who have shown their love by feeding the hungry, clothing the naked, and visiting the sick and prisoners shall be welcomed by the Lord of love.

"Not everyone that saith unto me Lord, Lord, shall enter the kingdom : but he that doeth the will of my Father which is in heaven."

NOTE

The further teaching of Jesus about the final coming of the kingdom almost certainly belongs to the period just preceding His death, and is best treated in that connection.

CHAPTER VIII

How the Pharisees received the Teaching of Jesus

WE must now see how the different classes of people received the teaching of Jesus, the good news of the kingdom ; and it will be convenient to begin with the Pharisees, because they were the most important people in the Galilean community.

Who the Pharisees were.

As a result of their continual subjection to the heathen nations a good many Jews had really lost faith in their God, and in the promise of the kingdom. There was a danger that an increasing number of Jews might give up the peculiar beliefs and customs that distinguished them from all other nations, and adopt the Greek beliefs and customs which were then followed throughout the Roman empire. This was a real temptation ; for it meant that they would have increased opportunities for trade, that their social relations with their conquerors would be far more cordial, and that they could enter the service of the empire, where their shrewdness would ensure them promotion.

The Pharisees stood for the extremest loyalty to Judaism, and especially to the law. Their object was to preserve the Jews as a separate nation until the time of the coming of the kingdom. In order to secure this object they tried to insist on a rigid obedience to the law in every minute detail, to ostracize all who did not adopt this attitude, and to foster a spirit of national pride at the expense of the heathen and Samaritans. As long as a Jew was faithful to the law he could not mix with Gentiles. He could not marry a Gentile. He could not feast with Gentiles, or assist at the worship of their gods. He could not even perform the trifling religious ceremony which was expected of every loyal subject of the emperor. He was a marked man. He alone was outside the comity of religion and culture that existed among all other subjects of Rome. His very circumcision exposed him to ridicule if he stripped to take part in the sports of a Greek gymnasium.

On the whole the Pharisees were popular, because they were the leaders of the patriotic party, the champions of religion, and because they kept alive the hopes of the nation. Their ancestors had been the most stalwart followers of the heroic Maccabees, which alone entitled them to respect; and their manner of life, their scrupulous observance of the detail of the law, their washings and prayers and alms kept alive this respect. At times men got rather impatient with their passion for detail; but in the main they were allowed to manage things pretty much as they liked.

How the Pharisees regarded Jesus.

Naturally enough the Pharisees were inclined to be critical when other people who were not Pharisees set up as teachers. They had been suspicious of John the Baptist, and they were even more suspicious of Jesus. Who was He? He was a mere nobody from some obscure Galilean village, a carpenter. What right

THE PHARISEES AND THE TEACHING

had He to set up as a teacher, when the scribes of the Pharisees had spent a lifetime in the study of the law and the tradition of the great rabbis?

The teaching of Jesus did not reassure them. It was said that He had actually had the blasphemous presumption to set Himself above the law that God had given to Moses. He was even reported to have used some such form of words as, " Ye have heard that it was said to them of old time, thou shalt not . . . ; but I say unto you. . . " To talk like that was sheer blasphemy; He was setting up to be greater than Moses. Here were they, learned and respected men, trying all they knew to keep the law and induce other people to keep the law, and then this ignorant carpenter gets up and preaches against the law. This low fellow starts to modernize the law of God, to say that it is inadequate, to expand it!

The worst of it was that He seemed to have got the ear of the people. There was some peculiar fascination about Him which attracted the common people. No doubt He had the gift of the gab. Also, being one of them gave Him an advantage. Still, one could not go against the people in these critical times. It was necessary to proceed with caution. If He were given rope enough, no doubt He would hang Himself before long. For the present the Pharisees must seem to suspend judgment, and watch carefully. When He betrayed Himself by some breach of the law, or some obvious heresy, they must expose Him ruthlessly.

So the Pharisees watched and waited.

They did not have to wait long. They soon heard that He was in the habit of consorting with the dregs of the people, with drunkards and harlots and apostates and publicans,—men so notoriously unfaithful both to their nation and to their religion that it was a sin to be seen speaking to them. It was a case of like calling to like. But now He had surpassed Himself. This imposter had a sort of staff, if you please—a band of men who followed Him about wherever He went, and were specially appointed. Most of them were low, uneducated men like Himself, fishermen and the like; but hitherto He had had the sense to choose men of fairly good character. Now, however, He had added to their number a publican—a fellow named Matthew or Levi, a man whose very trade proclaimed him an enemy of the nation, and a scorner of God. Verily the Lord had delivered this " prophet " into their hands! They heard that He was actually feasting in the house of this Levi—the self-styled " prophet of the Lord," carousing with the acknowledged enemies of the chosen nation and its religion! It was too rich!

Some of them went and stood round the house. A few of the " prophet's " admirers were there too. The emissaries of the Pharisees got into conversation with them. There was no need to say much. They just drew attention to the facts before them. The facts spoke for themselves. " He eateth with publicans and sinners," they remarked, with an air of mild surprise. " This prophet," they meant, " does what no respectable, God-fearing patriot would dream of doing. He feasts with the enemies of religion."

The admirers of the prophet had no answer. It was an amazing proceeding. They were frankly troubled and perplexed.

Their dismay was mentioned to Jesus as He sat at Levi's table. A smile crossed His features, in which, however, there was both sadness and indignation. How little His closest friends understood the

THE PHARISEES AND THE TEACHING 57

very elements of love ! How blindly prejudiced were His enemies, already on the watch to accuse Him ! He turned to His questioners, and said, "They that are whole have no need of the physician, but they that are sick : I came not to call the righteous, but sinners."

Many heard the saying, and it was eagerly discussed outside. The Pharisees were abashed. This carpenter was a clever fellow. They must be careful how they attacked Him. Moreover they recognized a certain sting in this apparently innocent answer. What said scripture? "There is none righteous, no, not one." What did He mean ? Did He imply that they thought themselves righteous when they were not ?

On the whole they thought it best not to renew the discussion, but to wait for some more favourable opportunity. Meanwhile they must go on watching.

A time of fasting came round. The Pharisees were fasting, and took care that everyone should know it. The disciples of John were fasting. But this prophet who feasted with publicans and sinners, what of Him and His disciples ? They did nothing of the kind. This seemed to call for explanation. It was worth while to ask the question. So they sent again, and asked, "Why do John's disciples and the disciples of the Pharisees fast, but thy disciples fast not ? "

And Jesus said unto them, " Can the sons of the bride-chamber fast while the bridegroom is with them ? "

What did this mean ? Who was the bridegroom ? Did He claim to be the Christ, or what ?

Jesus added, " No man seweth a piece of undressed cloth on an old garment ; else that which should fill it up taketh from it, the new from the old, and a worse rent is made. And no man putteth new wine into old wine-skins; else the wine will burst the skins, and the wine perisheth, and the skins: but they put new wine into fresh wine-skins."

Worse and worse! He apparently admitted that He was come to supersede the old religion with a new one, and was going to introduce new forms in which to embody it. His presumption took the Pharisees breath away. All that their ancestors had fought and toiled and died for was to be sacrificed at the bidding of this uneducated upstart, under the pretence of "fulfilling the law and the prophets." It was not to be borne.

Rumour reached them that He had even attacked their fasting as hypocrisy. "When ye fast," He was reported to have said to His followers, "be not, as the hypocrites, of a sad countenance: for they disfigure their faces, that they may be seen of men to fast. Verily I say unto you, they have their reward. But thou, when thou fastest, anoint thy head, and wash thy face; that thou be not seen of men to fast, but of thy Father which is in secret: and thy Father, which seeth in secret, shall recompense thee."

It was absurd. Was there to be no open religion? Was there no virtue in example? The Pharisees were furious; but what could they do? This fellow had bewitched the people, and they could not get a hearing.

At last they thought they had Him, for they had caught Him allowing His disciples to break one of the ten commandments. He had let His disciples pluck ears of corn on the Sabbath, and eat them. It was a flagrant breach of the fourth commandment. They went to Him straight, and pointed out the sin.

THE PHARISEES AND THE TEACHING

"Behold," they said, simply, "why do they on the Sabbath day that which is not lawful?"

Here was a dilemma. If He supported the action of His disciples, He stood self-convicted of being a breaker of the law that He pretended to fulfil better than anyone else. Had He not said, "Whosoever shall break one of the least of these commandments, and shall teach men to do so, shall be called least in the kingdom of heaven"? On the other hand, if He admitted that His disciples were in the wrong, why had He not rebuked them Himself? He would have to admit that the Pharisees were the more zealous.

Jesus accepted the challenge, but in a way that they little anticipated. He seized upon the incident to illustrate the whole difference in their attitudes. First of all He led up to the real answer by quoting a precedent. "Did ye never read," He asked, "what David did?" David, the national hero who could do no wrong, had broken the law when he and his men were hungry. He had even taken the shewbread, which it was not lawful for anyone but the priests to eat. Then, in a sentence, He summed up the whole position. "The Sabbath was made for man, not man for the Sabbath."

Here was the whole issue in a nutshell. Was the law an end in itself, or was it simply a means to an end? Was the law a tyrant, or a guide? Was the law made for man, to show him the road to God; or was man created to be the slave of the law?

The Pharisees were not prepared to confess their faith quite in this form. Once again the carpenter had turned the tables upon them. They had thought to put Jesus on the horns of a dilemma, and that was just where they found themselves. They slunk away in confusion, nursing their wrath against a future occasion.

The decisive battle was fought soon after. This time it was a pitched battle. The field was prepared, the spectators warned, and the combatants knew what to expect.

The question was still this one of breaking the Sabbath. Jesus had been healing on the Sabbath, and in the synagogue. This time there was no precedent that He could quote, and the issue was plain. The Pharisees therefore arranged that on the occasion of His next visit to the synagogue there should be a man with a withered hand present, as a test case.

The Sabbath arrived. The man with the withered hand was in his place. The Pharisees were present, reinforced by special deputies from Jerusalem. The curious thronged the building.

There was a hush as Jesus and His disciples entered. All eyes were turned on Him. Jesus looked round, and saw the man. " Stand forth," He said. Then, turning to His opponents, He made a final appeal to their common sense and charity. " Is it lawful," He demanded, " on the Sabbath day to do good, or to do harm ? to save a life, or to kill ? "

What could they answer ? The question was whether it was lawful to obey the law of love on the Lord's day. To say that on the Lord's day of all days it was unlawful to do a deed of love would be too absurd.

Jesus waited for their reply; but they were too proud and prejudiced to return the obvious answer. They held their peace. Jesus looked round with anger. He had tried to win them by appealing to their reason and their charity, and He had failed. Henceforth, in the interests of the common people,

THE PHARISEES AND THE TEACHING

there must be war between them. He turned to the afflicted man, and with love and pity and power in His voice, said, " Stretch forth thy hand." And the man stretched it forth, and it was healed.

The Pharisees were defeated, but they made a last attempt to prove their case. Whatever the man said, He had profaned the Sabbath, and shown Himself an enemy of religion. But the people were tired of the Pharisees. Their pride and narrowness had alienated the ordinary man, and he was glad to turn from them to Jesus who, by appealing to his reason and conscience and charity, had made religion mean something real to him. To the Pharisee he pointed out how good were the deeds of Jesus, how great His compassion on those who were sick and sorry, how wonderful His power over disease, and even over that most dreaded affliction which went by the name of devil-possession. Even the learned Pharisees from Jerusalem could find no answer to this. They lost their temper, and cried, " He hath Beelzebub," and " By the prince of devils casteth He out the devils."

It was reported to Jesus. First he pointed out the absolute irrationality of the accusation. " How can Satan cast out Satan ? " He asked. " If a kingdom be divided against itself, that kingdom cannot stand. And if a house be divided against itself, that house will not be able to stand. And if Satan hath risen up against himself, he cannot stand, but hath an end."

Then He went on to show the real significance of this power of His. To enter the house of a strong man, and spoil his goods, you must be stronger than he is, so as to bind him and then spoil him. Jesus was only able to prevail against the power of evil because He had in Himself the power which was stronger still—the power of God.

Finally He showed up the horrible blasphemy involved in this random charge of the Pharisees. It was not that they were wronging Himself; that did not matter. It was that they were calling good, evil. They were so blinded by their fury that they had lost all sense of right and wrong, and were calling the work of the Holy Spirit the work of devils. For men in that condition there was no hope. They had cut themselves off from all chance of salvation. They might be quite honest in thinking that He was an imposter, but to blaspheme against the Holy Spirit in the rage of their wounded pride was to deny the goodness of God. It was deadly sin.

This last mad accusation had made peace between Jesus and the leaders of the Jewish church impossible. For the moment the Pharisees did not dare take active measures against Him, because He was too popular; but there was no longer any secret about their hostility. All they dared do to discredit Him; to discourage men from following Him; to persecute His followers, they did. And they trusted to time to give them the victory. They knew the fickleness and instability of the crowd. Their turn would come, and then . . . then they would strike once and for all, and rid the world of Him !

CHAPTER IX

How the Common People received the Message of the Kingdom

IN every country and in every age it will be found that there is a tendency to callous selfishness and tyranny among the rich and noble; to legalism and artificial thinking among the moralists, ecclesiastics, and theologians; and to self-sufficiency and subconscious materialism among the well-to-do middle classes. The labourer, though often fickle and lacking in independence, is capable of a wider charity and a readier appreciation of moral and spiritual values than anyone else. Of course he has less to lose by altruism and idealism.

It will also be found that wherever there is cant and artificiality in the church of a nation, a great many honest and instinctively truthful people are driven to drink and various other deplorable forms of revolt against conventional respectability. Some people may think that England of to-day is no exception to this rule; but, be that as it may, Galilee in the time of the Lord Jesus was certainly not, and Jesus was heard gladly by publicans and sinners and harlots, and by ordinary simple-minded fishermen and peasants.

These publicans, of course, were tax-gatherers for the Herodian government, and for the Roman. For this reason they were classed as traitors to the nation. The pious Jews were convinced that as God's chosen people they had every right to be free; and to make one's living out of the fact that they were not was regarded as both impious and unpatriotic. The "sinners" were probably sinners primarily in the Pharisaic sense,—people who would not be bothered about the law. No doubt they were immoral as well; but they may easily have included some who were driven into a life of disreputability by the reaction of a jolly mind against the tedious formalism of the Jewish church. The peasants and fishermen were probably like most working-men of most ages, impulsive, lacking in constancy, emotionally patriotic and religious, and accustomed to endure the impositions of their "betters." They must have often chafed against the ecclesiastical tyranny of the Pharisees, but lacked the initiative to rebel against it.

To all these classes the teaching and personality of Jesus appealed in the highest degree. To those men and women who had long since made up their minds that they were predestined to damnation He gave a new hope, a new self-respect, a new confidence. The prophet treated them as spiritual beings, as beings who had value in the eyes of God. He talked to them, feasted with them, made them desire a cleaner life, and showed them how to set about making a fresh start. He offered them a picture of religion which was not cant, not self-satisfied, not narrow, and not artificial; but which, on the contrary, was the embodiment of the best sort of clean, vigorous, generous life. The courage and good deeds of Jesus, His freedom from conventionality and puritanism, His hard rough life, His direct simplicity and unswerving faith, His crisp incisive judgments, and the keen satire with which He crumpled up the sophistries of the legal mind—all these things appealed to sinners and plain folk, who were sick to death of the eternal wranglings of their religious leaders about tradition and precedent. And they were responsible for the inclusion in the circle of disciples of many men of a type which never before and never since have felt themselves welcome in religious societies.

Form of teaching.

At the same time Jesus fully realized that the fault of the common people was their lack of stability and independence. They were too emotional, too impatient. They would listen with wrapt attention, and immediately go off and forget. The parable of the Sower shows how well Jesus knew, that of the many who " heard Him gladly " very few made any serious attempt to carry out His teaching. For this reason He spoke in parables. The advantage of the parable is that it is easily remembered, and almost impossible to distort. Also, if its significance is not immediately understood, it rankles, and compels an individual effort of the mind. The ordinary sermon, however full of beautiful thought, is very easily forgotten. Its phrases tickle the ear, and produce a pleasing sensation ; but they have no enduring effect because they do not make a man think for himself. Probably, in most cases, the day after a really first-class sermon, half a dozen people who had heard it would agree that it was excellent ; but if they were able to give any account of it at all, the accounts would vary enormously. If, in the course of the sermon, a good simple story had been told, probably that would be the only feature on which all would be perfectly agreed.

The stories of Jesus were remembered, and would recur to the mind in the days following, stimulating thought about their exact significance, and having an effect that would be proportionately increasing and enduring according to the intelligence and earnestness of the hearer. Hence the saying, "To him that hath shall be given." History has abundantly justified this plan, for the stories of Jesus have lived, and proved of abiding value, and they are probably a great deal better understood now than they were at the time of telling.

At the time they were, as Jesus said, just seed. They sank into the minds of those who heard them, and, in some cases, lived and grew and burst forth into green blades and produced a harvest of good grain. But the period of maturing underground had to be gone through first, and the sun and rain of subsequent events had to do their share, and the effects of the sowing were not immediately apparent.

The chief effect of the teaching of Jesus at the time was to create the hope that He might prove something more than a teacher. The majority of the Galilean peasants would have been much more disposed to follow Jesus in a holy war than they were to follow Him in a holy life. They began to watch for indications of His ultimate purpose, and to speculate about the nature of His office. His healing power invested Him with a certain mystery. He was as much in advance of the average exorcist as He was of the average rabbi. Surely He was something more than a prophet! Might He not be the Messiah? The disciples began to think He might.

The people were naturally credulous, and rumours got about of wonders more marvellous than any work of healing. It was said that He had stilled a storm, walked on the sea. On one occasion, when He had distributed a few loaves among an immense crowd, so that each man only got the merest crumb, they had felt as satisfied as if they had had a full meal. A kind of craving for the miraculous sprang up. People followed Him about no longer to listen to His words, but on the chance of seeing a " sign."

The demand for a sign.

The Pharisees seized the opportunity to embarrass Him. " Oh yes," they affirmed, " if He gave a sign we too would believe in Him; but how can we accept the authority of a mere man as against the revelation of God, unless we receive a sign from heaven ? "

Jesus had long ago resolved not to demand a sign from heaven. In the wilderness, before ever He started to teach, He had thrashed that matter out. He realized that the time had come for Him to separate His most loyal disciples out, and to concentrate His attention on teaching them. He therefore withdrew from Galilee to a gentile country, and only those followed Him whose faith was established, and who were prepared to take some risks for the kingdom's sake.

NOTE

Crowds are always like this. They are impulsively generous, and capable of great achievements as long as the cause is successful. But they need rapid action and crude sensational oratory if they are to remain faithful to their leaders. Jesus would not pander to them. He would not sacrifice His high ideals, which, like all ideals that are worth anything, could only be attained by patience and grit, and at the cost of pain and danger. He would not pretend that what was hard was easy, that what must come slowly would be achieved in a moment, in order to retain the dubious support of the multitude. There have been many critics of the faults and hypocrisy of the powers that rule the world. There have been many champions of the people against their masters. There are still many of both types. But very few have kept their independence. If they have been free from the fear of tyrants, they have not escaped " playing to the gallery ";

and if by any chance a man has been free both of the classes and of the masses, he has seldom escaped the pit of pessimism and bitterness. Jesus, and some of the old Jewish prophets, alone succeeded in preserving complete freedom from illusions about human nature as it is, and yet remained optimists. It is doubtful whether it is possible to do this without intense belief in God. To be an optimist one must trust something or somebody, and if one accepts the verdict of the psalmist, which history seems to justify, and obeys the advice—

> Put not your trust in princes
> Nor in any child of man,

there is no alternative but to trust God. In the view of the Christian the resurrection and the history of the Church justify the optimism of faith which Jesus possessed.

It is easy to carp at optimism, and to talk about " the brave music of a distant drum "; but the fact remains that optimism is a necessity of healthy life, and that faith in God gives the only basis for optimism which has not been demonstrated to be unsound; which is in itself, perhaps, an argument for the rationality of faith. It is easy to say that faith is a dream, and that the idea of heaven is simply a drug to deaden pain; but there is no basis for optimism in physical science or practical experience, and yet we cannot produce good results without optimism. If optimism is necessary to progress it is likely to be truer than pessimism, and we must not jib at the implication that there is a God of nature, a purpose in life, a spirit in man, and a heaven in the future. To believe it requires intellectual humility; but we cannot afford to refuse the price.

CHAPTER X

THE DISCIPLES

JESUS chose twelve men to be His companions wherever He went, and to help Him in His work. Five of them were fishermen, and one a publican; the trades of the others are unknown. The chief of them seem to have been Simon, afterwards called Peter, and Andrew his brother; and James and John, the sons of a fisherman named Zebedee, who were nicknamed Boanerges, meaning sons of thunder.

These men saw all that Jesus did, heard all He taught, and were able to ask Him questions if they did not understand something. They more or less tried to control the crowds which followed Him about. If He wanted to cross the lake, they sailed Him across. The Pharisees brought their questions to the disciples; the women who brought their children to be blessed by Jesus had to run the gauntlet of the disciples first. Once they were sent out two by two to preach in the villages, and to prepare the way for their Master. The disciples had a pretty hard life, often sleeping out all night, and often going short of food; but they had a certain sense of importance in being attached to the person of so famous a teacher, and as long as He was popular their fidelity can be understood. But when people began to be impatient, and to ask who Jesus was, and what He was going to do, the apostles found themselves asking themselves the same question. They had left their families and their businesses to follow Jesus ; what was going to be the end of it ? John tells us that on one occasion, when men began to desert Him, Jesus asked the twelve whether they too would go away ; and Simon Peter answered, " Lord, to whom shall we go ? Thou hast the words of eternal life. And we have believed and know that thou art the holy one of God." The synoptists have a similar story. Mark tells us that as they went towards Cæsarea Philippi, Jesus asked them, "Who do men say that I am?" And they told Him that some said He was John the Baptist, some Elijah, and some one of the prophets. Then Jesus asked them, " But who say ye that I am ? " And Simon Peter answered, " Thou art the Christ."

This was the conclusion that His nearest disciples had come to, and if He accepted the title there would be no talk of turning back for His apostles. If He said He was the Christ, they would believe Him, and would follow Him through thick and thin. For the Christ would be the Lord of the kingdom of God, and His disciples would receive great honour therein.

This was a crisis in the life of Jesus and His disciples. His answer must have given Him as much anxiety as it did them. They wanted to know whether they were right in having given up everything to follow Him. Jesus felt certain that, as a matter of fact, He was the Christ ; but the question was whether He would be able to admit it to them without confirming all their wrong ideas about what being the Christ involved. He knew that if He confessed that He was the Christ, their minds would at once begin to dwell on the glories of the coming kingdom that the Christ was to found, and on their own place in it. He himself had developed new and entirely different views on the work of the Christ.

Would He be able to explain those views to them?

Jesus admitted that He was the Christ, and, while the disciples' hearts were lifted up with joy and pride, so that they were already beginning to anticipate the glory that would be theirs, He went on to tell them something of what He thought it meant. "The Son must suffer many things, and be rejected by the elders and the chief priests and the scribes, and be killed, and after three days rise again." And He spake the saying openly.

The disciples were amazed, bewildered. With one breath He had confirmed their highest hopes, and with the next He dashed them to the ground with words about death and suffering and rejection. "And Peter took Him, and began to rebuke Him."

From this time we find that Jesus devoted His chief energies to trying to prepare the minds of His disciples for what was to come, to eradicate their wrong ideas, and to get them to understand His point of view. That He failed is shown by the way that the disciples continually recurred to the subject of greatness in the kingdom; and by the fact that on His arrest every one of them deserted Him, and only Peter, and possibly one other, had the pluck to follow Him even afar off to His trial. That He did not completely fail is shown by the fact that after the crucifixion the disciples, though full of bewilderment and fear, still kept together, and whispered of the off chance that He might return from the grave. It will be convenient at this stage to consider what were the expectations of Jesus about His death, and about the coming of the kingdom after it.

There is no doubt that Jesus at this time looked forward to dying, and that He confidently expected that His death was going to set the seal to His work, was going to accomplish what His life had failed to do,—the founding of the kingdom of God with power. He had failed, and He knew it; though perhaps no one else knew it. People had thronged to hear Him. People had left all to follow Him. He had routed His critics at every encounter. He had cast out devils and healed the sick. He had done all that; but He had not planted the kingdom of God on earth. Only a few knew that He was the Christ, and even they showed how little they understood the nature of the kingdom that the Christ had come to found by quarrelling among themselves as to who should be greatest. Even James and John, the two disciples who, after Peter, were most faithful to Him, and shared His confidence in a special degree, came to Him to ask that they might sit on His right and on His left in the kingdom. To what purpose was His teaching about humility and service, or about the kingdom within, if even His closest friends remained consumed by ambition? He asked them if they were prepared to drink the cup that He must drink, and be baptized with the baptism with which He must be baptized, and they answered " Yes " with a glibness that showed how little they understood. Even so Jesus could not promise them what they asked. Though He was the Christ, though His death was, He was certain, the prelude to the coming of the kingdom with power, though in that kingdom He would be glorified, and His faithful followers recognized; yet the kingdom was the Father's. Jesus knew not the hour of its coming, knew not for whom the chief honours were reserved. Jesus was acting all through in faith. He knew that He was called upon to die. He knew that His death was going to be

THE DISCIPLES

efficacious in bringing in the kingdom. He knew that in the end the kingdom would be perfect, and God be all in all. He knew that His disciples must be prepared to suffer even as He was going to suffer. But more than that He did not know, and He was content not to know. What He knew was sufficient for Him. He knew what to do, and He knew that His work was to stand ; and more than that He felt that, as man, He had no right or occasion to know.

This was where Jesus was so pre-eminent. He had the courage to act on faith. His faith was so real that it was effective. Other men have faith in the abstract, and it comes on top at moments. The faith of Jesus was on top all the time, and He saw that that was the one sort of faith worth having, the one sort of faith which was not hypocrisy. Unless one was prepared to risk everything, even life itself, one's faith was a mere pretence. "He that would save his life shall lose it ; but he that loseth his life for my sake and the gospel's, the same shall find it." Jesus was going to bring matters to a crisis. He was going to compel His disciples to take His words seriously. He was going to let His enemies seize Him. He was going to undergo every humiliation that men could inflict—spitting, mocking, flogging, and finally exposure naked upon the cross. He was going to be held up to the public view, amid every circumstance of ignominy that man could devise, as an accursed thing, as "crucified carrion." His disciples were going to be left without a hope. They were to see all their false hopes of a worldly kingdom dashed to pieces. All their greed for power and honour was going to die in their breasts. They were going to be left with one thing only, their only really valuable possession, their love for Jesus. Then they would realize its value, and the Father would do what He would do. Jesus did not know exactly what that was. He knew that His death would not be the end, for He felt within Himself the life which is eternal. He knew that He would rise from the dead, and that, in His own time and in His own way, God would show to the disciples that their faith and His was justified.

In their lifetime the disciples would see His glory. They would see the kingdom come with power. When they least expected it, their Lord would return. Let them watch continually, pray continually.

Then they would understand the truth. Then, when all their illusions had been crucified upon the tree, and they were left with nothing upon which to build them afresh, they would believe that the kingdom was a spiritual kingdom, and that the gods of the world were false. Then they would be compelled to believe in the heavenly Father who was above all human standards of wisdom and goodness and power. Then they would lose their fear of men, their fear of death and shame and every other fear with which men are afraid, and would become free and able to enter the kingdom. Then the kingdom of God would have been established upon earth, and would spread all over the world. The old dispensation would be at an end. Jerusalem would fall at last, and finally; and the place of the Jews who had refused the kingdom would be taken by the Gentiles. Last of all the final realization of the kingdom would take place; the wheat be finally separated from the tares and the chaff. All that was worthless and harmful should be finally destroyed, and all that there ever had been of good, clean life brought together and made into an eternal kingdom of God.

CHAPTER XI

JERUSALEM

ACCORDING to St. Mark the excursion into the region round Cæsarea Philippi which was mentioned in the last chapter was followed by a secret visit to Galilee, and from there Jesus went to Judaea and beyond Jordan. There the crowds once more assembled round Him, and probably some rumour of His claim to be the Messiah reached the crowd in spite of His injunction to the disciples to keep silent about it. Anyhow, when He started towards Jerusalem there seems to have been a large company of enthusiastic Galileans with Him, who made His journey something of a triumphal progress. It was at this time that Peter said, "Lo, we have left all and followed thee," as if to draw from Jesus some definite promise of reward; and Jesus is reported to have replied, " There is no man that hath left house, or brethren, or sisters, or mother, or father, or children, or lands, for my sake, and for the gospel's sake, but he shall receive a hundredfold now in this time, houses, and brethren, and sisters, and mothers, and children, and lands, with persecutions; and in the world to come eternal life." It was at this time that James and John preferred their request to sit on His right and left hand in the kingdom, and were told, "whosoever would be first among you shall be the servant of all." As he entered Jericho the crowd was so great that a little publican named Zaccheus, who wanted to see Jesus, had to climb a tree. The popularity of Jesus had suddenly returned with redoubled force, and the reason evidently was that He was reported to have accepted the title of Christ, and that His visit to Jerusalem was regarded as significant of His intention to take active steps to found the kingdom. Luke says that as they approached Jerusalem the multitude thought that the kingdom was immediately to appear, and that Jesus told them the story of the " pounds " to show them that the Christ had got to depart for a season first.

The climax was reached when, near the villages of Bethany and Bethphage, Jesus sent for a colt, and rode into Jerusalem, while the Galilean following spread garments and branches in the way, and shouted, " Hosanna ; blessed is he that cometh in the name of the Lord : blessed is the kingdom that cometh, the kingdom of our father David : Hosanna in the highest."

There is no mistaking the meaning of this cry. The kingdom of David was Jewish, temporal, and warlike. It is hardly to be doubted that in the expectation of the crowds the kingdom of Jesus was to be a similar affair. Some, if not all, of the apostles probably shared this expectation, notably, if one may hazard a guess, Judas Iscariot.

The authorities at Jerusalem were disturbed. They had heard of this prophet before, and some time previously the Jerusalem Pharisees had sent down a commission to Galilee to examine His claims, and to quench His influence if it appeared to be pernicious. They had ended by declaring that He was possessed by Beelzebub, and had a vivid recollection of their defeat at His hands, which made them chary of bandying words with Him.

The Sadducees, or priests, were equally perturbed. They were not a religious body, and did not believe in the resurrection, or long for the coming of the kingdom. They strongly resented any activity which was likely to give Pilate, the Roman governor, an excuse to interfere in the affairs of the city, and perhaps curtail their powers, or extract money from them. The arrival of a prophet with a noisy and turbulent Galilean following who believed Him to be the Christ was about the most undesirable event that could happen from their point of view.

Almost the first action of Jesus was a direct challenge to the priests. He took it upon Himself to drive out the money changers and the sellers of animals and birds for sacrifice from the temple precincts. He arrogated to Himself the right to deal with a matter which was under the jurisdiction of the priests. And yet so popular was He, and so justifiable His action if He was a prophet, that the priests could not very well interfere without causing a riot. They therefore began to seek means to destroy Him secretly, before He had also bewitched the inhabitants of Jerusalem, and the other visitors to the feast.

Jesus, meanwhile, came to the temple every day to teach, and retired to Bethany in the evening to lodge. On the return journey He very often used to go to a garden on the mount of Olives for meditation and prayer, and His apostles went with Him. This seemed to offer the only chance of seizing Him, for it was the only time when He was near enough to Jerusalem, and sufficiently alone for it to be possible to do so without raising a riot. But before His enemies could do this, they must have everything prepared. They must make sure of not seizing the wrong man in the dusk, they must have a charge ready to bring against Him, and witnesses to prove it; and nothing but a capital charge would suffice. The whole business must be carried to a finish before there was time for His disciples to take action.

The first care was to formulate a charge; and with this object an unholy alliance between the Saducees, the Pharisees, and the followers of the court of Herod was formed, with a view to entangling Him in His talk. Herod was in Jerusalem at this time, and it is quite possible that the reason why Jesus hurried through Galilee on His return from Cæsarea Philippi was that He had been warned that Herod was on the look out for Him, and intended that He should share the fate of John the Baptist. It was not that Jesus was afraid to die, but that He felt called to die at Jerusalem.

The Herodians and the Sadducees may have been on fairly good terms already, for they both belonged to the lax section of the population; but that the Pharisees should have associated themselves with these inveterate foes shows how bitter was their resentment against Jesus.

The object of these allies was to induce Jesus to admit that He claimed to be the Christ, and that He intended to oust the Romans, and establish a Jewish kingdom in Jerusalem. They thought Him sufficiently a demagogue to be unwilling to sacrifice His influence with His Galilean following by definitely repudiating such an intention; and if He admitted that He was a rebel against Rome, they could force Pilate to execute Him.

The first question was put by the chief priests, and doubtless referred to the purging of the temple court of traffickers in animals. They demanded to know,

JERUSALEM

"By what authority doest thou these things?" Jesus saw that it was simply a trap, and saw no reason why He should play into their hands; so He refused to give them an answer unless they would first tell Him whence they imagined that John the Baptist got his authority. This was equivalent to saying that Jesus got His authority from the same source as John, and implied that His action in cleansing the temple was an action which John was quite capable of performing, and for the same reason. Jesus had not yet made any such explicit claim to be the Christ as could be twisted into a ground for a charge of treason or blasphemy, and He intended to choose His own time for doing so. The priests were discomfited. They dared not answer His question, and so He refused to answer theirs. But turning to His disciples He told them a story about the absentee Lord of a vineyard, whose servants were one by one killed by the men to whom he had entrusted its management, and who ended by even laying hands on his son. This story was a scathing condemnation of the descendants of Zadok, the so-called Sadducees, who had rejected every prophet that God had sent; and also implied in terms that would be recognized by the followers of Jesus, that He Himself was something more than a prophet.

The next question was put by the Herodians and Pharisees, and was whether it was lawful to give tribute to Cæsar or not. They pretended to be the friends of Jesus, and tried to imply that He had only to say the word and they would follow Him in His war of liberation. The Pharisees were patriots, and Herod pretended to be one at times. But Jesus had had experience of the "friendly" overtures of the Pharisees, and was not to be caught. His answer,

"Render unto Cæsar the things that are Cæsar's, and unto God the things that are God's," might mean anything. It might mean that He was no rebel; but some would interpret it otherwise, seeing in Cæsar a usurper of God's throne. But it was no basis for an accusation, and gave no opening for further discussion. It put the onus of interpretation on the questioners.

The plot had failed so far, and the enemies of Jesus desisted from their attempts to bandy words with Him. At dialectic He was their master, and invariably made them fall into their own pit. Meanwhile, however, the followers of Jesus were getting somewhat impatient. They had not come to Jerusalem to talk, but to act. One day, as He was leaving the temple, someone called His attention to the magnificence of the temple buildings, and Jesus answered, "Seest thou these great buildings? there shall not be left here one stone upon another, which shall not be thrown down." This saying was widely reported, and caused serious misgiving. It was reported to the priests, and they were both incensed and excited. Could they not turn it to account? It certainly seemed that the prophet had been indiscreet. How would the Galileans like it, for instance? And could it not be made the basis of a charge of blasphemy? It was true that blasphemy was hardly a capital charge, but if they had the people on their side they might be able to force Pilate's hand.

The disciples of Jesus were also perplexed. Peter, James, John, and Andrew formed themselves into a deputation to ask an explanation. They came to Him on the Mount of Olives, and asked, "When shall these things be?" Then follows a long rambling discourse in Mark, which has been considerably altered in Matthew and Luke, and is not very reliable in detail. Nevertheless it probably contains elements which were genuinely present in the teaching of Jesus, though probably neither He nor His disciples were very clear as to the exact order of events. Jesus foresaw His death, followed by a period of persecution for His followers, through which they would be strengthened by the Holy Spirit. He foresaw a period of political unrest, in which many false Messiahs would rise and further inflame the ambitions of the Jewish populace. This could have only one end—the fall of Jerusalem. That would mark the end of the old dispensation of the law, and the new dispensation of the kingdom would then begin with power, and the gospel should be preached to the Gentiles, since the Jews had rejected it. This dispensation of the kingdom would end in a final destruction of evil, and the Christ would return to reign over an eternal kingdom of goodness. This kingdom would not be of this world. The present order of nature would come to an end, the stars fall, the sun and moon be darkened. The kingdom would be of " the world to come," a world in which the faithful dead would live again.

The teaching of Jesus about the end of the world, as given in the gospels, is not very consistent; and the reason probably is that the disciples tried to interpret it in a much more definite and detailed way than Jesus intended, and to make it fit in as far as possible with their preconceived ideas on the subject. It is hard to believe that Jesus ever used the commonplaces of " apocalypse " quite as He is represented as doing in Mark xiii., for His teaching generally has a very distinct individuality, and shows a strong commonsense which seems to be lacking here. Also it is impossible to think that the apostles could have remembered such a long, complex discourse word for word. Nevertheless it is practically certain from the parables of the " pounds," the " ten virgins," the " marriage feast," the " vineyard," etc., that Jesus did look forward to the conversion of the Gentiles, the fall of Jerusalem, the persecution of the Church, and the final realization of the kingdom in heaven—a realization in which all His faithful disciples would share, and He Himself play a leading part.

The effect of this discourse cannot have been altogether encouraging to those who still cherished a hope that David's kingdom was about to be restored. The apostles had followed Jesus partly no doubt from love, but partly also in the hope of reaping a rich reward for their infidelity. The growing realization that their reward was indefinitely postponed, and that it was to be preceded by a time of stress and trial, was unpleasant for all of them ; and they still hoped against hope that it would not be so. Still, for most of the apostles, withdrawal was now impossible. They loved and trusted Jesus too much to be able to leave Him in His hour of trial. But one of them, Judas Iscariot, was apparently so chagrined by his disappointment that he determined to hasten on a crisis. He went to the chief priests and offered to betray his Master. It is hardly possible to doubt that in doing so he was not altogether sordid, and that he desired to force the hand of Jesus, and perhaps of God. His faith had failed him. He could not go on any longer trusting without some sign. But, as he arranged his dastardly conspiracy with the enemies of Jesus, he probably hoped that Jesus would yet confound them, and perhaps would even live to thank him for what he had done.

The plan adopted was the only one that offered any chance of success. Jesus must be seized when almost alone, and when far from help, and late in the evening, when His followers would have dispersed to the suburbs. He must be tried and condemned that same night, and in secret. The next day He must be hurried to Pilate as early as possible, and with any luck the whole affair would be over before the people had had time to take action. Probably the priests did not altogether take Judas into their confidence.

Jesus knew of the plot; but made no attempt to evade arrest. He felt that His hour had come, when He must give His life "a ransom for many." He and His disciples met as usual for supper in an upper room that they had been lent during the time of the feast. It was not the passover meal, as the synoptists represent, but on the evening before that on which the paschal-lamb was slain. Jesus told the apostles that He was to be betrayed that night, and bade Judas go and do that which he had planned. Then, after supper, He took bread and broke it and gave it to them, and said, "this is my body." And He took a cup and made them drink of it, and said, "this is the new covenant in my blood." And He told them to continue this ceremony when He was gone. It was a covenant between Him and them, that when He was gone He would still be their Lord, and that they would still be faithful to Him and to each other. It was a symbol of unity, the unity of the one body in which every part shares the common life, so that all are one.

Then, when they had thus sworn loyalty to Him and to each other, they sang a hymn, and went out to the Mount of Olives, to a garden called Gethsemane. As He went, Jesus warned them that He was going to be taken, and prophesied that all would be scattered. The disciples reiterated their love and fidelity, and their readiness to die with Him if necessary. Peter, as ever, was the foremost; and Jesus said to him that before cock-crow he would have denied his Master.

When they came to the garden, Jesus took Peter and James and John ahead, and then, bidding them watch, went still further Himself, to pray. Jesus was very sad. He hated the thought of all that He would have to go through. There was no cowardice in this. Everyone who is not morbid and unwholesome dislikes the sordidness of a trial, and Jesus knew that His trial would involve every detail of degradation that His enemies could contrive. He would be seized by the priests' guards, bound, hurried off to a secret trial which would be a mockery of justice. He would be condemned, treated with ignominy and contempt, spat upon, buffeted, mocked. He would be deserted by all His followers. Then, at dawn, He would be hurried to Pilate, a weak man, who would be jockeyed into crucifying Him. He would be stripped and scourged by the soldiers, and then hurried off to Calvary, the place of execution. There He would be stripped naked, and exposed upon a cross till He died, a public spectacle, a thing of contempt. Helpless He would hear the triumphant mocking of His enemies, and worse still, the amazed despair of His friends. All that He had lived and worked for, all that He had achieved, would seem to end in nothing. It was not a prospect which any healthy-minded man could contemplate without disgust and revolt. The cruelty and sordidness of it were repulsive. Yet Jesus did not flinch. If it was necessary, He was ready to go through with it.

He believed that it was necessary. As far as He could see it was the path which God had marked out for Him to follow. If so, He was content. Nevertheless He prayed that it might not be necessary. "Father, all things are possible to Thee: remove this cup from me: nevertheless, not what I will, but what Thou wilt." It was the prayer of One who was neither a morbid fanatic, nor a coward; but a brave, faithful, wholesome man, a loyal and heroic Son of God.

CHAPTER XII

The Death of Jesus

Three times Jesus came back to the three apostles whom He had left to watch, and each time He found them asleep. The third time He heard the sound of the soldiers in the distance. The time for watching was past; the time had come when sleep was as good as any other course. He went to meet His enemies, and Judas greeted Him with a kiss, crying " Hail, Master." It was a sign, and the soldiers seized Him. He expostulated with them for their violence. He was not a robber. He twitted them with being obliged to come and seize Him by violence, and at night, when He had been peaceably teaching in the temple every day.

He was hurried off to the High Priest's court, which had been assembled in readiness, and His disciples fled incontinently. Afterwards Peter turned, and followed secretly.

The witnesses and judges were waiting, and the trial began. Unfortunately, they could not trump up a capital charge. Jesus remained silent. There was no point in His making a defence. He watched the witnesses contradicting each other, and the growing impatience and baffled fury of the High Priest. It was an undignified proceeding, this assembly of proud hierarchs trying in vain to find some plausible excuse for condemning One on whose death they had decided for the simple reason that He was too truthful, too full of the burning Spirit of God to be endured by the representatives of an effete formalism. It was not the business of Jesus to save their dignity from humiliation. No amount of circumstance could grace this solemn farce with the dignity of a court of justice.

At last the High Priest, in desperation, turned to Jesus and challenged Him: " Art thou the Christ, the Son of the Blessed ? " he demanded.

Jesus answered, " I am : and ye shall see the Son of man sitting at the right hand of power, and coming with the clouds of heaven."

It was characteristic that Jesus should choose this moment for the first plain and public assertion of His claim. Just at the moment when escape was impossible, when His disciples had fled, demoralized, when He was bound and helpless in the hands of His enemies, when there was nothing before Him but a shameful death, when His words could have no effect but to play into the hands of His enemies—this was the time to make the solemn declaration that He was the Christ, and that the kingdom was His ; this was the time to show His belief that God really was God, and above every human standard of power and thought.

The High Priest was amazed and delighted. He had probably anticipated another of those baffling answers with which Jesus knew so well how to turn the tables on His foes ; but no, the time for dialectic was past. The time had come for the issue to be plain between them. The answer of Jesus was the challenge of faith. He said in effect, " Take me, do everything that you can to degrade and humiliate me, kill me ; nevertheless, you are fighting an unequal battle, you are fighting against God. I am the Christ, and you will admit it hereafter."

"What need have we of witnesses ? " asked the High Priest. " Ye have heard the blasphemy, what think ye ? " And they all pronounced Him to be worthy of death. Then, as was fitting, at the close of such a trial, they spat on Him, and, blindfolding Him, hit Him, and said " Prophesy, who was it that smote thee ? "

Meanwhile, Peter was in the courtyard below, and a maid accused him of being one of the followers of Jesus, and he denied it. Three times he denied his Lord, and then the cock crew, and Peter, remembering the prophecy of Jesus, went out, and wept bitterly. Peter was demoralized ; but his love he could not help. He had seen the shattering of all his hopes ; but he retained what, though he did not yet know it, was the one possession of any value, his love.

Then followed the dawn, and the trial before Pilate. It is unnecessary to go through the whole painful story ; it is plain enough in the gospels. Pilate was forced against his will to order the crucifixion. He hated the priests ; but he also feared their influence at the imperial court. Jesus, having been dragged about and maltreated all the night, was scourged by the soldiers ; and the Roman scourging was a far more terrible ordeal even than the lashes which we English abolished not so very long ago in the navy and merchant service as being brutal and degrading. The Roman scourge was loaded with lead. Then He was mocked by the soldiers of Pilate. They thought it a good joke to mock "the king of the Jews." Then, half fainting, He was compelled to carry the heavy cross of wood to the place of execution outside the city. Naturally, He fainted from sheer exhaustion, and the soldiers compelled Simon of Cyrene, the father of Alexander and Rufus, to carry it for Him.

THE DEATH OF JESUS

Alexander and Rufus, who were they? Perhaps it was the Rufus that St. Paul greets in the epistle to the Romans. Anyhow, they must have been proud in after years to be the sons of Simon of Cyrene, who bore the Lord's cross for Him. Yet, at the time, who would have expected that to be such a claim to fame as to secure that their names should be handed down to an infinitely remote posterity?

Jesus was stripped, and nailed to the cross, and raised to display His agonies to the public, with a thief on either side.

Mark only records one sentence as spoken from the cross, a sentence which seems at first sight like a cry of despair. "My God, my God, why hast thou forsaken me?" Yet when one realizes that it is the opening sentence of the twenty-second psalm, in which it almost seems as if the poet had seen a vision of the figure upon the cross, and which, though it begins on a note of despair, ends on a note of faith and confidence, even that bitter cry seems only the cry of One who was enduring the supreme test of faith and felt that He had plumbed the lowest depth of that which He was set to endure. Luke records that when the soldiers nailed Jesus to the cross, He prayed, "Father, forgive them, they know not what they do"; and that when one of the thieves turned to Him and, after confessing that he was suffering only what he deserved, said, "Jesus, remember me when thou comest into thy kingdom," Jesus answered, "To-day shalt thou be with me in Paradise." Luke also records, as the last words of Jesus, "Father, into thy hands I commend my spirit."

So, just about the time when the paschal lamb must be slain, Jesus gave up the ghost; and hastily His body was buried near the place where He died, that it might not remain upon the cross during the Passover Sabbath. Judas, seeing the outcome of his action, went and hanged himself; the priests and Pharisees went home, half frightened at the success of their plot; and the disciples went to their upper room or their lodgings to pass the feast day in despair and shame and fear that their turn might come next.

CHAPTER XIII

WHAT HAPPENED AFTERWARDS

JESUS was dead and buried. Perhaps the Pharisees and the chief priests hugged themselves at the thought that at last the pestilential carpenter was finished with. They did not attack His disciples, or worry about them. They had smitten the shepherd, and the sheep were doubtless scattered. Anyhow, not a hand had been raised either to defend Him or to avenge Him, except that Malchus, the servant of the High Priest was said to have lost an ear, and had it put on again by the "prophet."

Nearly six weeks passed, and still there was no sign of existence shown by the Galilean's faction. No doubt the sect was broken up, and had dispersed home to Galilee, where Herod could be trusted to deal with them. They would not dare appear in Jerusalem again for some time after the sharp lesson they had had. There were rumours. . . . There always are rumours. And the Pharisee and the priest laughed fatly.

Then suddenly Peter reappeared in Jerusalem. After lying low for nearly six weeks, Peter and all the rest of the pestilential crew suddenly appeared in Jerusalem, and openly started to preach. But what on earth had they left to preach? Had not the whole city seen their "Christ" die a felon's death, an accursed death, the most damaging sort of death possible, upon the cross? What was this nonsense?

"Ye men of Israel, hear these words: Jesus of Nazareth, a man approved of God unto you by mighty works and wonders and signs, which God did by Him in the midst of you, even as ye yourselves know; Him being delivered up by the determinate counsel and foreknowledge of God, ye by the hand of lawless men did crucify and slay: whom God raised up, having loosed the pangs of death: because it was not possible that He should be holden of it. . . . This Jesus did God raise up, whereof we all are witnesses. Being therefore by the right hand of God exalted, and having received of the Father the promise of the Holy Ghost, He hath poured forth this, which ye see and hear. . . . Let all the house of Israel therefore know assuredly, that God hath made Him both Lord and Christ, this Jesus whom ye crucified."

Such was the "nonsense" preached by St. Peter, as recorded by St. Luke; and strange to say, such was the conviction and power with which he spoke that thousands believed him, and were baptized, and continued steadfastly in the apostles' teaching and fellowship, in the breaking of bread and the prayers.

But who had seen Him, and where, and when?

He had been seen at intervals during forty days ever since the day after the passover. He had been seen first by Peter, and by two who walked to Emmaus, one of whom was Cleopas. Mary Magdalene had seen Him. The eleven remaining apostles had seen Him more than once. Five hundred brethren at once had seen Him. James had seen Him. He had been seen both in Jerusalem and in Galilee.

Was He the same?

Yes, even to the print of the nails in His hands and feet, and the wound of the soldier's spear in His side

WHAT HAPPENED AFTERWARDS

Had He spoken to them?

Yes, and He had shown them from scripture that the Christ must die, and He had sent them to preach in His name to all people, and had given them the gift of the Holy Ghost.

But what about the tomb? Wasn't His body still there?

No, when the women went to the tomb after the passover to embalm His body, they found the tomb empty, and until they saw Him they feared that the body must have been stolen.

Was He in the body then?

Yes, and yet it was different. It was a spiritual body. It looked just the same, and yet He could appear and disappear at will.

But where was He now?

He had taken a final leave of them, and they had seen Him disappear into the clouds of heaven. But His presence was always with them, though unseen; and when they died, or He returned to judge the world, they would see Him again.

Many more details were given in answer to such questions, and perhaps they were not always quite right or quite consistent, and perhaps as time went on the story became embellished with details that were quite without foundation; but, however that may be, the thing which convinced people was the absolute and unshakable conviction of Peter and those that were with him, and the evidence of power that they gave in their boldness and preaching and works of healing. It was and is very difficult to believe that it rested on a basis of fancy and illusion.

The chief priests tried to prevent them from preaching; but they would not be prevented. They were imprisoned, and they escaped, and reappeared in the temple court. They were beaten, and told to desist; but they would not desist, and rejoiced that they were accounted worthy to suffer for the Name. Stephen was stoned, James was executed, a zealous young Pharisee named Saul went round seeking victims. But the Church flourished, and Saul was converted, and became Paul, having seen Jesus in a vision. The apostles were obliged to flee from Jerusalem, and they scattered to Antioch, and Joppa, and other places, making fresh converts wherever they went. Within thirty years there were churches all over Asia Minor and Greece, and even in Rome itself. Within about forty years Jerusalem had been destroyed, the Jews dispersed finally and for always, the old dispensation of the law was past, and that of the kingdom begun " in power."

PART II

THE CHURCH: ITS IDEAL, ITS FAILURE AND ITS FUTURE

With special reference to the Church of England; being the orthodoxy of a heretic, and the catholicism of a Protestant.

CHAPTER I

DEFINITION OF THE CHURCH

"I RECEIVED of the Lord that which also I delivered unto you, how that the Lord Jesus in the night in which He was betrayed took bread; and when He had given thanks He brake it, and said, This is my body, which is for you; this do in remembrance of me. In like manner also the cup, after supper, saying, This cup is the new covenant in my blood: this do, as oft as ye drink it, in remembrance of me."—
1 Corinthians xi. 23-25.

"As the body is one, and hath many members, and all the members of the body, being many, are one body; so also is Christ. For in one Spirit we were all baptized into one body, whether Jews or Greeks, whether bond or free; and were all made to drink of one Spirit. For the body is not one member but many. If the foot shall say, Because I am not the hand, I am not of the body; it is not therefore not of the body. And if the ear shall say, Because I am not the eye, I am not of the body; it is not therefore not of the body. If the whole body were an eye, where were the hearing? If the whole were hearing, where were the smelling? But now hath God set the members, each one of them in the body, even as it pleased him. And if they were all one member, where were the body? But now they are many members, but one body. And the eye cannot say to the hand, I have no need of thee: or again the head to the feet, I have no need of you. Nay, much rather, those members of the body which seem to be more feeble are necessary : and those parts of the body which we think to be less honourable, upon these we bestow more abundant honour ; and our uncomely parts have more abundant comeliness ; whereas our comely parts have no need : but God hath tempered the body together, giving more abundant honour to that part which lacked ; that there should be no schism in the body ; but that the members should have the same care one for another. And whether one member suffereth, all the members suffer with it ; or one member is honoured, all the members rejoice with it. Now ye are the body of Christ, and severally members thereof."—1 Corinthians xii. 12-27.

"Even as we have many members in one body, and all the members have not the same office : so we, who are many, are one body in Christ, and severally members one of another."—Romans xii. 4-5.

"And He gave some to be apostles; and some, prophets ; and some, evangelists ; and some, pastors and teachers ; for the perfecting of the saints, unto the work of ministering, unto the building up of the body of Christ : till we all attain to the unity of the faith, and of the knowledge of the Son of God, unto a fullgrown man, unto the measure of the stature of the fulness of Christ : that we may be no longer children, tossed to and fro and carried about with every wind of doctrine, by the sleight of men, in craftiness, after the wiles of error ; but speaking truth in love, may grow up in all things into Him, which is the head, even Christ ; from whom all the body fitly framed and knit together through that which every joint supplieth, according to the working in due measure of each several part, maketh the increase of the body unto the building up of itself in love."—Ephesians iv. 11-16.

" I am the true vine, and my Father is the husbandman. Every branch in me that beareth not fruit, He taketh it away : and every branch that beareth fruit, He cleanseth it, that it may bear more fruit. . . . As the branch cannot bear fruit of itself, except it abide in the vine ; so neither can ye, except ye abide in me. I am the vine, ye are the branches : he that abideth in me, and I in him, the same beareth much fruit : . . ."—John xv. 1-5.

" By this shall all men know that ye are my disciples, if ye have love one to another."—John xiii. 35.

The meaning of the definition.

" The Church is the body of Christ." This means that the Church, which is an association of a large number of men and women, who differ from each other in race and language, and qualities and occupation and temper, has got to embody the personality of Jesus Christ. Its members have got to remain different, just as the members of a human body are different ; but they have got to be parts of a single life, to be obedient to a single will, and to combine with each other so as to carry out the purposes of that will, just as the members of a healthy and well-controlled human body do.

The business of a body is to express a personality. Through the body a personality makes itself heard and felt and understood, carries out schemes, and gets into touch with other personalities so as to understand and be understood by them. So the business of the Church is to enable Jesus Christ to make Himself heard and felt and understood in the world, to carry out His work of giving to men the knowledge of

God and so freeing them from the tyranny of false ambitions and passions and fear, to give Himself to men and to receive from men their love and obedience.

If a man's body is inefficient he cannot make himself understood, or get into touch with other men. If he is blind and dumb and deaf and crippled and insane, his personality remains shut up out of the world. So with Jesus Christ, unless His body the Church is healthy, He cannot make Himself understood by men, or carry on His work in the world, or get into touch with men at all. He remains unknown, except as a person in history, like Cæsar or Socrates. So we churchmen have got to try and make the Church healthy, and until we can do that, our Lord will not be able to increase the kingdom of God on earth.

Now in the body of a man there are many members, and each member has a desire for its own development and gratification. The organs of sex have desires that demand satisfaction. So have the appetite and the palate. The muscles want to be strong, and demand to be practised. The mind wants to grow, and asks for instruction. The eyes and ears clamour to see and hear beautiful things. And the badly regulated body is the one in which some particular member has got what it wants at the expense of the rest. For instance, some men are simply sexual animals, and their muscles and mind are sacrificed to the satisfaction of the organs of sex. Other men are drunkards, and nothing else. Others are only learned, and have big heads but weakly bodies. Others again are simply strong, and have no knowledge or sense. Others spend all their time looking for beautiful pictures and scenery, and listening to beautiful music, and have no kindness or strength or usefulness. But men who are developed in one direction like this are never as efficient, even in that direction, as the man who is developed all over. The sexual man will not beget such fine children as the man who is also strong in his body and gentle and wise in his mind. The drunkard will never have such good taste in wine as the moderate drinker, or enjoy his drinking so much. The opinions of the scholar, no matter how many books he may have read, will never be sound and useful if he has a bad digestion and a diseased liver. The muscular man cannot be a good boxer and gymnast, or even a capable workman, unless he has sense and a brave heart and a knowledge of human nature.

So in the body each member gets the best out of itself by working as a part of the whole body, and in co-operation with the other members, and not by simply going for its own desires. The members of a body are healthiest and most efficient when they are all obedient to and controlled by a single will for the accomplishment of a single purpose. And so, according to Christianity, it is with men and women. They do not get the best out of themselves by selfish greed, but by working in loving fellowship with their neighbours, as a great family whose interests are the same, which includes all ages and nations and classes, and whose father is God. And if there is a God this must be true. If there is a creative life-giving Will in nature, happiness and full development can only be got by living in harmony with that Will. And if that Will desires the ultimate good of every man and woman, *i.e.*, if God is love, men and women can only be happy by seeking the good of mankind, and by giving up their own desires when they interfere with the good of others. And if there is no God, it is perhaps best to be a cynic, for then one will be in harmony with a meaningless and purposeless nature.

But Christianity takes its stand on the love of God, and even goes a step further. It says that Jesus of Nazareth was a man who was a true Son of God, who lived His life in perfect obedience to the loving will of God, and that therefore He was the perfect man. This means that the personality of Jesus was in perfect harmony with the will of God, and that His personality had perfect control of His human body. It means more than that. It means that the personality of Jesus, which once showed the will of God through the human body that was born of Mary the Jewess, could also show the will of God through any other human body, and that His personality is the sum of all the goodness of all the men and women that ever have been or ever will be. Christianity says that if men and women can embody in their own lives the personality which was once revealed in Jesus, they will become the best that they are capable of becoming. And Christianity says that all men and women can to some extent embody the personality of Jesus, because He is alive and not dead, and through prayer and the sacraments they can receive the Holy Spirit which will make them one with Him. Christianity says that just as the members of a body are living and useful when the blood circulates freely through the veins, and makes them part of one single life, and just as the members of a body are numb and dead if the valves are choked up, and the circulation of the blood impeded; so men and women are living and useful when they are animated by the Spirit which was in Jesus, and are dead and useless when the Spirit does not make them alive.

According to Christianity the personality which

DEFINITION OF THE CHURCH

was once shown to men in the body of Jesus of Galilee is the all-embracing personality of the Son of God, the Lord of all good life. And through the Church men and women are to come into touch with Him. The Church is to be His body, in which He still lives and works and speaks, through which He still proclaims the love and forgiveness of God, opening men's eyes to the vision of God, freeing them from the forces of corruption, and giving them the good and eternal life that comes from God.

It is as if a master played a melody on a wonderful violin, and then an orchestra under his direction tried to play the same melody on a large number of instruments. They would not play in unison but in harmony; and until the players had all arrived, and had caught the spirit of the master, and were dominated by him, their playing of the melody would be discordant, and would in every way do it less justice than the master's playing on the single instrument. But in the end, if they tried loyally each to play his own part in harmony with the rest and in perfect obedience to the will of the master, the final result would be a far fuller rendering of the melody even than the original playing on the one violin. And in that perfect harmony each individual player would have got much more out of himself than if he had played alone.

So in the world of men and women. Jesus is the master who once played the melody of heaven on the single instrument of His human life in Palestine; but the same melody needs for its perfect rendering the combination of all men and women playing each on the instrument of the life that God has given, in perfect obedience to the Master whom God has sent to conduct them.

The Church is the body of Christ. At the centre the great heart of Christ still beats strongly, pumping the life-giving blood into the veins of the different members ; but unfortunately the valves are choked up, the blood cannot circulate freely, the members fail to work in harmony with each other, and many seem numb and dead.

CHAPTER II

PROTESTANTISM

English Protestantism.

Jesus was the friend of simple men, and also of sinners. He was the stern critic of the rich and the respectable, because, though they obeyed the conventions and laws and traditions of men, they missed the beauty of the holiness of God. Though they were respectable, they were not humble and generous and free and charitable.

Now if we look at English Protestantism we find just the same fault that Jesus found in the Pharisees of old. Speaking generally, it is the rich and the respectable that are found in church and chapel. Men and women who have sinned against the conventions and traditions of society are not welcome there. People who are too poor to buy decent clothes are looked askance at if they attend public worship. Simple people very often cannot understand or follow the services. What is required of the good Protestant is that he should be honest in business, moral in his private life, reasonably generous in supporting the funds of the church or chapel to which he belongs, and regular in his attendance at public worship. He should also have " the assurance of salvation," and shake his head over those who have not. But, after all, this is very much like the description of the Pharisee in Jesus Christ's story of the Pharisee and the publican. The Pharisee was not an extortioner or unjust, nor was he an adulterer; he fasted twice a week, and gave to the temple a tenth of all he got. He thanked God that he was not as other men. Yet Jesus said that he got no good from his prayers—not so much, in fact, as the publican, who was so conscious of his sins that he dared not so much as lift up his eyes, but stood afar off, and said, " God be merciful to me a sinner."

It is to be feared that very few Protestants get much good out of their worship, and for the same reason —that they are lacking in humility, and have made the same mistake of confusing respectability with holiness. It is to be feared that Jesus Christ would not feel very much at home among English Protestants, and that He would be likely to slip away from them, as He did of old, to sup with those who did not pretend to be good at all, and yet were simpler and more generous and more able to understand Him than the men who thought themselves good. Indeed, this is what our Lord Jesus has done; for you will often find a more truly Christian spirit of fellowship and generosity, and a better understanding and appreciation of the character of Jesus, in the street than in the churches and chapels.

· In short, English Protestantism fails to embody the personality of Jesus Christ, fails to show Him to the world, that all men and women who want to be better may go to Him for help, fails to do His work of healing and freeing mankind. There are Christ-like Protestants in England : there are whole congregations which embody Him; but they are like a vigorous little toe at the end of a great numb, and paralysed foot. The English Protestant churches as a whole are a very dead limb of the body of Christ.

The origin and root idea of Protestantism.

Protestantism is very ancient. It dates from the time of the apostles. From the time of the crucifixion of Jesus right up to the conversion of the Emperor Constantine, nearly 300 years later, the Church of Christ was Protestant. That is to say, it was an association of small scattered groups of people, who were trying to live pure, unselfish, holy lives in the midst of a pagan society, which was full of open cruelty and immorality. They were trying to be the light of a very dark world. Amidst hatred and persecution they tried to keep up a high standard of brotherhood and holiness. And in the struggle for existence they were obliged to exclude from their ranks those who were notoriously immoral, or who had dealings with idolatry. The force of circumstances forced them to be a little narrow and intolerant and exclusive.

The question is whether this ideal of the Church, as a little band of saints trying to be the light of a very dark world, can be applied in England to-day, and the answer is that it cannot. To begin with, the English nation, though one would hardly describe it as godly, is certainly not godless. There is not a single Englishman whose ideas of right and wrong are not influenced by the teaching of Jesus. In the abstract almost everyone admits that public spirit, independence of character, purity of life, unselfishness, generosity, humility, and brotherly love are the right ideals. The conscience of Jesus Christ is really the supreme moral guide of Englishmen, though they may not always admit it. This being the case, the attempt to separate the saints who are saved from the sinners who are damned has led to the application of external tests of an artificial kind. Whether we admit it or not, in practice the churches and chapels apply the following tests to try and sift the wheat from the chaff :—

The test of orthodoxy—whether one believes the creeds.

The test of respectability—whether one obeys the laws and the conventions of society.

The test of loyalty—whether one attends certain services or not.

The test of clothes—whether one has a Sunday suit.

These tests are wrong. They do not pick out the saints and exclude the sinners. Only God, who sees the heart, can do that. The only effect of these tests has been to make the Church in England narrow and formal and hypocritical. We have made the same mistake as the Pharisees, and turned what was meant to be a help into a burden. The Bible, the creeds, the Prayer Book, were all made for man, not man for them; but just as the Pharisees sold themselves into slavery to the law, so we have sold ourselves into slavery to the Bible and the Prayer Book, and the creeds, and have missed the freedom of Christ. We have also made the other mistake of the Pharisees, and confounded respectability and morality with holiness. Respectability is a purely conventional thing, defined by artificial standards laid down by men. Morality is a result of holiness, but it is not holiness, and may exist without holiness. Mere morality is negative, holiness is positive. Morality is ice, holiness is fire. Morality is conventional, holiness is beautiful. Morality is self-satisfied, holiness is humble and aspiring. Morality is of the world, holiness is in the world, but of heaven. Morality can be reached, holiness is infinite and eternal. Morality is not doing wrong, holiness is trying to be good. Morality is governed by reason, holiness by love. "... if I ... know ... all knowledge; ... and if I bestow all my goods to feed the poor ..." I am moral all right, specially if I do the bestowing through the Charity Organization Society; but according to the apostle of Christ, "if I have not love, it profiteth me nothing."

No, morality is not holiness, and English Protestantism is not Christianity; it is much too respectable. If we are to make our Church a more living limb of the body of Jesus Christ, we must make it more Catholic. We must get in the lame and the poor and the sinners and the harlots, and lots of simple, straightforward working men, specially carpenters and fishermen. And if necessary we must make a scourge of small cords and drive out the rich and the learned and the conventional. And if necessary we must "destroy the temple," burn down the cathedrals and churches, and retire to upper rooms and gardens, and deserts and boats. We hope it may not be necessary; but at whatever cost we must make room for the Master, and remove all the things that keep Him from us.

There may have been, in fact there probably was a time in the history of the English, when Protestantism was as necessary and as feasible as in the days before the conversion of Constantine; but that day has passed. In the days of the Roman Protestants the Church was small and poor, and its members were many of them slaves and people of humble origin, and it was persecuted. So, too, was the Protestant section of the Church in England in the old days when the king and the bishops and the magistrates were all opposed to it. In those days it was possible for Jesus to dwell in Protestantism. But now, when it has become rich and powerful and respectable, Jesus has disowned it.

CHAPTER III

CATHOLICISM

The meaning of the word Catholic.

The word catholic means through all. When applied to the Church it means that it must include everyone, and fill all whom it includes with the spirit of Christ. There can be only one body of Christ, and there can be only one Catholic Church. But there may be many limbs in the body, and many parts in the Church. Nevertheless, all parts must act as a part of a whole, or all will suffer.

The Church became Catholic after the conversion of Constantine, for then the whole Roman world began rapidly to follow the example of its emperor, and profess Christianity. The work of the Church immediately changed. It could no longer aim at being a small society of keen people trying to keep up a high ideal in a corrupt and hostile world. It had to make the world part of itself, clean it, fill it with life, help it to find its best self in the body of Christ. The body of Christ had suddenly shot up; and as with a quickly growing child, there was a danger that its energy and character and vitality would suffer. It had new possibilities, new responsibilities; but there was a danger that the body would be less firmly knit together, and the different members less under control. And as a matter of history the Church developed certain weaknesses at that time from which it has never since entirely recovered.

Weaknesses of Catholicism.

BISHOPS

To begin with, the bishops of the Church became very important people, specially those who lived at the capital cities, Constantinople and Rome. They became courtiers and diplomatists, and caught a greed for money and power. And so the Bishop of Rome still sits enthroned in a palace, as ruler of a petty kingdom, and is surrounded by intriguing diplomatists in red hats. So, too, our English bishops live in " palaces," are addressed as " my lord," sit in the House of Lords, and have to "keep up the dignity of their position." Of course, individuals realize how absurd it is for the head shepherds of Christ's flock to set store by outward honours and position, and think longingly of " Monseigneur Bienvenu " in Victor Hugo's *Les Miserables;* but the tradition started in the reign of Constantine is too strong for them. The Church has become worldly, and is no longer free.

DOGMA

Another weakness was due to the fact that a lot of rather second-rate philosophers, who had hitherto confined their attentions chiefly to the Greek philosophies and Oriental religions, started to explain Christianity. They were generally not very good Christians, and just looked on the faith as an intellectual problem. Up till that time Christianity had, in the main, been an attempt to live a spiritual life, and what creeds there were were simply statements of the facts of experience on which that life depended. For instance, the Christians knew that through the man Jesus they got into touch with God. They found God in Him. He was God's Son. And through contact with Him, their lives became quite different. Their weakness and fear and snobbishness and greed disappeared. They knew that the change was not brought about by their own strength. They knew that it was the Holy Spirit, the Comforter, whom Jesus had promised, that made them new men. So, in their creeds, they just said what they knew—that they believed in God the Father, and in Jesus Christ His only Son—the man that Pilate crucified, and who rose again. And in the Holy Ghost. There was no philosophy about this—nothing to argue about. It was either true or not true; and from their own experience they were willing to bet their lives, even in the circus, that it was true. But now these philosophers came along and asked conundrums. How could Jesus be God and man ? How could the Son of God suffer ? How could the Father, Son and Holy Spirit all be God, and yet there be only one God ?

If the Christians had been wise they would have stuck to their guns and said, " We can't know all about God. We can only know what God has chosen to tell us. We know that so much is true, and if you try to work it out in practice you will find that it is true. But exactly how it ought to be put philosophically we neither know nor care." Unfortunately the Christians tried to argue, with the result that they argued for about 200 years, when the barbarians came and stopped them. But meanwhile the faith had got tied up in little fifth century boxes, like the Athanasian Creed. We have never stopped making dogmas and arguing about them. Roman Catholicism has added the immaculate conception of the Virgin, and the infallibility of the Pope to the faith in quite recent years; while many Protestants would have liked to enunciate as a counterblast the infallibility of the Bible, which, indeed, is practically made part of the creed by the wording of the ordination service. Anyhow, even the English Church has never escaped from the Athanasian Creed, which is a document of unknown origin. In fact, all that is definitely known about it is that it was certainly not written by Athanasius, and that no council ever launched it as a creed.

The practical result of this philosophizing of Christianity is that even now Christians are taught so many things that have no relation to experience or life, that they generally forget the things that have. Also for a hundred years or so both Roman Catholicism and English Protestantism have been fighting scientific truth in the interests of obsolete theology, thus disgusting all who love the truth for its own sake, and turning men's attention from their heavenly Father and their Master His Son to such subjects as the behaviour of the sun on the occasion of a battle that may or may not have taken place about 3,000 years ago, and whether a fish that Peter once caught had a coin in its mouth or was sold for a coin.

MASS

Again, whereas Jesus Christ, on the night that He was betrayed, instituted a symbolic service which was meant to define for ever the meaning of His Church and the ideal of His disciples, the converts who swarmed into the Church at the conversion of Constantine must needs bring in their own superstitious ideas. They did not in the least want to be members of Christ; but they wanted to take part in the mysteries and magic of the new religion. And so in time came the doctrine of transubstantiation, which means that just as when the pagan priest

CATHOLICISM

mutters an incantation over the idol of his god the spirit of the god enters the idol, so when the Christian priest mutters an incantation over the bread and wine they become the body and blood of Christ. The only good thing about the Roman mass is that, even under the cloak of superstition, it does bring home to the worshippers the presence of their Lord, which is more than can be said for sung matins at eleven.

THE CUP

From this followed the refusal of the priests to offer so precious a thing as the blood of Christ to the laity, specially to such a laity as were the new converts of the age of Constantine.

LATIN

Since Holy Communion had become a bit of magic, it did not matter much what language was used; and so to this day the incantations of the Roman Church are said in Latin, which is not always understood even by the priest; and in this way the understanding of the real meaning of the service is still further hindered.

ABSOLUTION

Further, it is probable that the Roman doctrine of priestly absolution also dates from the time of Constantine. We have said in the first part of this book that we believe that Jesus preached that God forgives as soon as a sinner repents, and that the meaning of forgiveness is that God is ready to help. Evidently it will make a tremendous difference to a sinner to know this. If a man has sinned and is full of shame and sorrow, and thinks that God has ceased to love him or hear him, he will despair. But if he knows that God still loves him, and is willing to help him, he will have the power to mend. Therefore the declaration by Jesus "thy sins are forgiven" was effective in saving the sinner from despair, if he believed that Jesus knew. The pronouncement of forgiveness by Jesus did not alter God's attitude to the sinner, it altered the sinner's attitude towards God, and made him take advantage of the fact of God's love and forgiveness. Just as Jesus is always present in those who love Him, but the sacrament of the bread and wine enables them to realize the fact more than at any other time; so God always forgives the sinner who really repents, but the declaration by the priest in Christ's name of this fact brings the fact home to the sinner, urges him to real repentance, and enables him to count on God's love in fighting temptation. This, we think, the true meaning of "priestly absolution," and surely it is the view of the Church of England; but the Roman Church, and certain advanced English churchmen seem to preach the to us impossible doctrine that God does not forgive until the priest gives the word. One explanation of this custom of priestly absolution is as follows: Before the conversion of Constantine the Church had been obliged to exclude from communion people who fell into such sins as adultery and idolatry, and before being readmitted to communion they had to make a public confession of their sins in the presence of the whole congregation. After the conversion of the court of Constantine the number of these confessions became so great that the congregation delegated the duty of hearing them to the priest.

However the custom arose it has certainly had very bad effects. The Roman Catholic is often not at all troubled about leading a good life if he thinks that he can get absolution before he dies. The system has only one advantage, and that is that it makes the sinner feel that he has a right to be in the Church, and there he may come to love the Master. The difference in this respect between Roman Catholicism and English Protestantism might be summed up by saying that the message of Romanism is, "If you can't be a saint, be a sinner, and get absolution," while that of Protestantism runs, "If you can't be a saint, be a Pharisee." Surely the message of Christ was, "If you can't be a saint, try, and God will help you to succeed."

SAINTS

Finally, the pagans who came into the Church would not give up their ancient shrines and images and festivals; so these were "Christianized" by turning the gods into saints. It is said that there is still a shrine in Sicily dedicated to "Santa Venera" on the spot where once stood a shrine of Venus.

SUMMARY

To sum up, the charge against Catholicism is that in trying to include the world it became worldly. The limbs of the body of Christ which are called "Catholic" seem to be paralysed by the bandages of superstition and magic and language and philosophy and greed and worldly arrogance and power. But the bandages are dropping off from sheer old age, and unless new ones are woven the great "Catholic" limb of the Church may yet gain freedom of movement and real power.

CHAPTER IV

PROTESTANT CATHOLICISM

WHAT is wanted is that the Church should be both Protestant and Catholic, that it should both shame all kinds of sin, and include all men and women who want to be good. The Church ought to include everyone that wants to be better than he is, and it should hold up an ideal which, in embracing all good life, shall inspire love and devotion and faith in Christ among all different kinds of people.

If Jesus is not a universal personality, the Lord of *all* good life, the Church had better shut up shop. If, on the contrary, the Church holds to its opinion that He is just that, let it try to cease to be narrow and artificial.

The conditions which must be fulfilled by a Catholic Church.

The Church has the following chief duties: worship, teaching, fighting, saving, and unifying. If it is to be Catholic it must help *every* type of man and woman to worship, teach in such a way as shall allow freedom of growth to *all* truth, fight *every* false god and *every* force that makes for disease and death, show a way of freedom to *all* imprisoned souls, and unite *every* bit of good life in the body of Him who is the Lord of *all* good life.

The Church in England.

We must now go on to see how these principles can be or are applied in England, and the moment one mentions England one realizes what a very complicated problem it presents from the Christian point of view. In England there are three distinct ideals of Catholicism represented. First the national Church of England claims to be the true Catholic Church in England. Its ideal is that each nation should have one Christian society, including every Christian in it ; and that all these national societies should be self-governing members of a world-wide federation which should be the Catholic Church. All these societies should have certain common features which should secure their unity. They should be governed by bishops consecrated in one and the same way : the same sacraments of holy communion and baptism should be administered by priests ordained in one and the same way, and explained in one and the same sense. The same creeds should be the definition of belief for all, and the same Bible the ultimate source of authority under God. The different churches of the one federated Church should recognize each others' members, priests, bishops, and sacraments ; and questions affecting the whole Church should be settled by councils of bishops. This is the ideal of the Church of England, and it was also the ideal of the ancient Church. It will be found, for instance, in the letters of Ignatius, who was martyred early in the second century.

Unfortunately the Church of England has not succeeded in including all the English Christians in its borders, and in failing to be in fact the Church of the whole nation, it has failed to be in fact the Catholic Church in England. Also it has failed to agree with the Churches of Rome and of the East, and to realize its ideal of federation with them.

Secondly there is the Roman ideal. This is similar to that which we have just described, except that instead of a federation the Romans desire an ecclesiastical empire ruled by the Pope of Rome. The Roman Church has failed to be more than a small sect in England, owing to its superstition and narrowness.

Thirdly, there is the " Free Church " ideal, which would have a federation of Churches in one Church, but disowns the safeguards of unity desired by the Church of England. The Free Churches will not admit the necessity of uniformly consecrated bishops and uniformly ordained priests, nor indeed of any external tests or safeguards at all. Unfortunately, the Free Churches have also failed to be Catholic, and perhaps more than any other Christian body have fallen into the pit of Pharisaism.

In the following chapters we shall try to discuss what should be the ideal of the Church of England, which is in a sense the connecting link between Protestantism and Catholicism; and to discover in what way it can best prepare the way for an ultimate Catholic reunion. It will be found that there are two courses open to it. By sacrificing the ancient safeguards the Church of England could immediately secure an external union with the Free Churches, and realize the idea of a national Church; but in doing so it would lose all possibility of linking up with the Roman and Greek Churches. The second course open to it is to try to enlarge its borders so as to make Dissent unnecessary, while at the same time keeping the safeguards which should make worldwide reunion ultimately possible. It is in this direction that we believe that the English Church should try to move. There is a third alternative—to stay exactly as it is. But this is surely a counsel of despair, for at present the English Church fulfils none of the conditions required even of a national Church.

CHAPTER V

Catholic Worship

THERE are three principal services in the Church of England—Holy Communion, morning prayer, and evening prayer. We must consider each of these, and see how far they can be reasonably expected to help every English man and woman who wants to be better to worship the God who can make them better. But first of all it will be a good thing to get clear in our minds about the object of public worship. We must realize at the start that the Prayer Book was made for man, and that it has to serve certain purposes, and that if it fails to serve those purposes it must go, be it never so ancient and venerable.

The object of Holy Communion.

The object of holy communion seems to be to symbolize the two ideas which lie at the root of all Christianity: that the Church is the body of Christ, and that the members of the Church are members of Christ. At holy communion the worshipper ought to realize just what it means when he calls himself a Christian. It means that in loving fellowship with his brother Christians he is pledged to try loyally to embody the personality of Jesus Christ. The Master is to come first in his life, to dominate it. The Master's work is to be his work, the Master's ideal to be his ideal, the Master's Spirit to be his spirit. Forgiven himself, he is to forgive others. Loved himself, he is to love all men. Strengthened himself, he is to strengthen his brethren. As Jesus suffered for him, so he is to suffer for others. In so far as in him lies, and in co-operation with all other men who love his Master, he is to try to reproduce the life of Jesus Christ. And in so far as he really tries, Jesus Christ helps him and strengthens him with the Holy Spirit. There at the holy table the Christian realizes in a moment all that his life is meant to be, and all the forces which are ever ready to help him. The forgiveness of his sins, the presence of the living Christ, the gift of the Holy Spirit, the fellowship of the whole Catholic Church—all these are his, and at the supreme moment of communion they are all really present to him, under the wonderfully all-embracing symbols of the bread and wine.

The object of Morning and of Evening Prayer.

Then, at morning and evening prayer, come the more prosaic elements of worship, and they are arranged in the Prayer Book services in a beautiful order. First comes humble sorrow and confession because we have failed, followed by the declaration that if we are really sorry we are forgiven, and that God will help us to do better. Then, in the gladness that follows forgiveness, come songs of rejoicing and praise and thanksgiving. These are interrupted for a few moments by instruction from the Bible, to remind us that the best thanksgiving is a holy life built on the solid foundation of the example of our Master and His saints. Then comes a great time of intercession, when we pray for all that is of interest to us, for peace among nations, for good government for the Church and its ministers and people, for judges and prisoners, for rich and poor, for the sick and the dying, for children, for the heathen and the sceptics, for the hypocrites, for everyone in all the world. The great time of prayer is interrupted once by the note of praise which must still prevail, and closes with thanksgiving and benediction. It is in its intention a beautiful service, and may well serve as a guide in considering what worship ought to be.

Criticism.

Having appreciated the services of the Prayer Book, we must pass to criticism, and ask why it is that people do not as a matter of fact find in them the beauty that is there.

Holy Communion.

To begin with, we have the Romans on the one side complaining that we miss in our service the whole point of holy communion which, according to them, is the conversion of the bread and wine into the body and blood of Christ; while the Dissenters on the other complain that by having a specially ordained priesthood and a set form of service we are destroying the simplicity which is essential. To the Romans we can give no satisfaction. We must trust to time to prove which of us is right; but the contention of the Dissenters needs careful consideration. We must be quite clear about the object of an ordained priesthood and a uniform service. The English Church always has its eye on the future and on the possibility of a universal Church. Supposing such a Church to exist, it would be almost essential that Christians should be able in every part of the world to take part in the great service of Catholic fellowship, the service

CATHOLIC WORSHIP

of holy communion. It is a beautiful idea that wherever a Christian should go in all the world, and in whatever strange language his brothers in Christ might be worshipping, he should always be able to follow this one service, and find it the same everywhere. After all, holy communion, enshrining as it does the essence of our faith, is the obvious basis of unity. And there seems to be no good reason why, as we all come to understand its meaning more fully, there should not in this one thing be uniformity. Therefore the English Church has tried, as far as possible, to keep to the old form of service in which, from very ancient times, the rite of the breaking of bread and the drinking of the cup has been set. Besides this, the set form of service and the specially ordained ministry are a certain guarantee that the meaning and beauty of the service will not be lost. If it were to be celebrated anyhow and by anybody there would be grave danger that false interpretations might creep in, and important features allowed to drop out. In this matter we think that the Church of England would not serve the cause of ultimate catholicity by sacrificing what seems to be beautiful and useful for the sake of an immediate unity which would mean the impoverishment of the future. Not by giving up what is beautiful and good, but by including more of what is beautiful and good, will the Church of England substantiate its claim to be Catholic.

At the same time the Prayer Book service might be improved. To begin with, the ten commandments are supposed to stand for a test by which the Christian is to judge his conduct. They are a very clumsy test. We do not want to make graven images nowadays, we don't keep Saturday holy, and we don't believe that God said He made the world in six days. Moreover, the Christian has to go far beyond the righteousness laid down in several of the other commandments. In all books of preparation it will be found that the ten commandments are only made useful by representing them as bearing a meaning which on the face of them they do not bear, and it would surely be much better to substitute for them parallel words of Christ on the lines followed in the first part of this book, or to use the beatitudes or the " two great commandments."

Then the arrangement of the service, with the exhortations and special prefaces coming right in the middle, and the epistles and gospels somewhere behind, seems to make it unnecessarily difficult for simple people to follow.

Finally, the language might be translated into more modern English in some parts, without really altering its order or meaning, to the great benefit of uneducated people, whom Christ no doubt would wish to be able to follow everything.

Morning and Evening Prayer.

Morning and evening prayer are much more liable to criticism. They have the same faults of language which are characteristic of the whole Prayer Book, and many others besides.

The chief fault is not in the intention of the service, but in the fact that the various parts do not fulfil that intention. It is a beautiful idea that the declaration of forgiveness should be followed by songs of praise : but the songs chosen, the psalms, very often fail to express anything which can have any meaning on the lips of a Christian congregation. Surely we have something more recent to praise God for than the victory of the Israelites over Og the King of Bashan, and Sihon, King of the Amorites. There seems no reason for using the psalms in this unintelligent and haphazard way. If certain particular psalms were picked out and apportioned to Sunday use it might be that nothing better could be found; but the only result of the present system is that hardly have people entered church than they are set to do something which they cannot do intelligently, and they therefore fall into a sort of comatose condition, which often lasts till the end of the service, and utterly destroys the possibility of real worship. We make the worship of God of none effect through our tradition.

The same criticism applies with equal force to many of the lessons. The idea of having lessons here is good, but the lessons so often teach nothing. This indiscriminate use of scripture seems to have arisen as a result of the pernicious doctrine that all scripture was equally inspired and edifying, and that if it wasn't it ought to be.

It is difficult to say whether, if the psalms really did praise and the lessons really did teach, the canticles would seem more relevant; but at present, with the exception of the beautiful song of Simeon at evening prayer, they do not seem to grip. Even the song of Simeon seems to be rather misplaced, for it is a little premature to sing " Now Lord lettest thou thy servant depart in peace " when the service is not half over.

The prayers and the litany and the versicles seem to belong to an age that is past. The King and the Royal Family and the nobility and the dynastic wars seem to occupy a place which is quite out of proportion to their actual importance in the State;

while the Cabinet and the House of Commons and the permanent officials and the municipalities and the employers of labour and the sweated workers, all of whom need our prayers very badly, hardly come in at all.

If morning and evening prayer are to mean anything definite to the majority of English men and women, they must be brought into closer touch with actual life. They must be made more incisive and relevant. They must really praise, really teach what we all need to be taught, really pray for the people and things that do count in our lives. It is impossible to doubt that they could be so reformed as to keep their beauty of intention and order, and at the same time be made intelligible to even the simplest of God's children; but until that is done the simple will stop away from church because they do not understand what is going on, and the educated because they find the services insincere.

Other Services.

But a much bigger question needs to be raised. Is it possible that one form of service, however good, can be expected to suit all the different types and classes of people that go to make up the Church of England; and if not, is it justifiable for a Church which only provides one form of service to pretend to be the Catholic Church of the nation? There are so many different temperaments in a nation that it is difficult to believe that uniform worship is even desirable.

In a large town in the north of England there are some very terrible slums. The houses are mean and overcrowded, stuffy and ill-ventilated, the streets are narrow and filthy, there is a general air about the district of cramped and stunted life, and sordid discomfort. It is difficult to see how people living in such a place could be expected to have any idea of God, or any purity or idealism of soul. On a Sunday morning you can step straight out of these streets into a spacious church. The high vaulted roof gives a feeling of bigness and nobility. The fragrance of incense replaces the odour of garbage and filth that pervades the street. The swelling tones of a great organ reverberate majestically through the echoing aisles, in strong contrast to the raucous stridency of the barrel organ outside. Boldly but artistically coloured pictures decorate the walls, telling the story of Him who died that we might have more life. The altar is lit up with a hundred lights, and there the priest, in stately robes, is consecrating the symbols of the body and blood of One in whose presence the first are last and the last first. And all the great church is full of people. There are the poor widows with their mites, the blind and the lame, the poor and oppressed, finding hope and courage and self respect and courage in the Fatherhood of God and the fellowship of Jesus. There are the rich and the well born learning to despise riches and honour, and to seek eternal treasure and love at the foot of the cross of the Prince of Glory. Is there not room for something of that sort in the Catholic Church of a nation?

Again, in another mean district of another great city you will find seventy poor working boys crowded into the upper room of an old warehouse, singing hymns, and listening to simple lessons and prayers and addresses for love of the same Lord. Is there not room also for this? For neither of these congregations would come, perhaps, even to a reformed morning prayer or evensong.

People who love colour and sound and smell want to put these things into their worship of God, and have they not the support of the author of the book of Revelation ? Others find these things merely distracting. They find that they can best think of God in the plainest and most severe surroundings. All human magnificence seems to them out of place before the throne of God. Yet both types must be included in the Catholic Church.

Surely in addition to morning and evening prayer there ought to be some great ritual service, symbolizing, perhaps, the idea of the Church as the body of Christ, just as the simple early communion seems to accentuate the idea that we individually are members thereof. And surely, too, there ought to be room for extempore prayer and simple " gospel services " for those who are hardly advanced enough in learning to appreciate the more carefully beautiful services of morning and evening prayer.

Whether such " gospel " services should be as rigidly marked out in the Prayer Book as the present ones, or whether there should be a greater liberty allowed to individuals ; whether they should be controlled entirely by the clergy, or entrusted to the laity, is a question which it is difficult to answer. But if the Church is to enlarge its borders to include all the men and women of England who love its Master, and if it is going to make dissent and the reluctance of the poor inexcusable, they must be introduced. And with this greater liberty to diversity must go a stronger insistence on the importance of holy communion as the service of unity, a saner and simpler and more intelligible teaching of its meaning, and a simplification of the liturgy.

NOTE

The respective merits of set forms and extempore prayer.

The advantage of set forms is that the congregation is less at the mercy of the mood and spirituality and sincerity of the minister. Services which are entirely extempore are apt to lose the quality of worship. Prayer is apt to degenerate into preaching with one's eyes shut, and thanksgiving into exhortation to gratitude. Also if the minister is not in the right mood he may very likely become unctuous and insincere in the attempt to make an effect.

On the other hand, set forms are very apt to become mere forms, and to lose the quality of heartiness.

CHAPTER VI

CATHOLIC TEACHING

It is evidently the first duty of the Catholic Church to teach the religion of Jesus Christ. In the first part of this book we have tried to show that the religion of Jesus consisted in a belief in the fatherhood of God, which belief, when accepted without reserve, produced a new outlook on life, a new idea of the relative importance of the things that make up life, and a new freedom and beauty of character. This, surely, is what the Catholic Church has to teach—how to realize the fatherhood of God, how to regard the problems of life, how to regard our fellow men, how to tell the relative value of the different ambitions and desires which arise in our hearts, how to use all the many faculties which we possess to accomplish the best of which we are capable. The great question is whether our present methods of education are at all calculated to teach this simple, definite, and practical religion. We are compelled to admit that they are not. It is notorious that the majority of those who have received a " Christian education " have very vague ideas of what Christianity is. Their faith is easily upset, they are easily led away by the more practical if fantastic doctrines of " Christian Scientists " and Theosophists, they are easily driven into scepticism by the crudest attacks on what secularists imagine to be the Christian faith.

The writer was reading not long ago a popular

attack on Christianity. This book gave him the following general idea of what its author imagined Christianity to be:—

(1) A belief that Jesus was the Son of God because He is said to have been born of a virgin, to have performed miracles, and to have risen bodily from the grave, and ascended bodily into heaven.

(2) A belief that the Bible is in every respect true, in all its historical, scientific, and moral statements.

(3) A belief in the thirty-nine articles.

(4) A belief that those who profess to trust in Jesus Christ will be saved from their sins by His sufferings upon the cross, and that those who do not will perish everlastingly.

Most of us will probably agree that this is a caricature of Christianity; and yet to the writer's certain knowledge hundreds of people who imagined themselves to be Christians have accepted this man's definition of their faith, and have allowed him to demolish it for them. Similarly, when travelling in the steerage of a liner, the writer heard a group of Christians utterly discomfited by the crude attacks of a retired butler on such matters as the swallowing of Jonah by the whale, the morality of King David, and the authorship of the " Books of Moses." These men had had a " Christian education," and yet they felt that if Moses did not write the book of Leviticus, and Jonah was not swallowed by a whale, the very foundations of their faith were shattered! Whose fault was it? Surely that of the Church which taught them so badly.

Too often the education of Christian children consists of an indiscriminate teaching of the old testament, which leaves the impression that it is to be regarded as verbally inspired; a similar teaching of the new testament; a teaching of the ten commandments as the basis of morality; and a teaching of the creeds in a parrot-like, and wholly unpractical way. Only too often the principle which governs Bible teaching is, "Don't tell the truth until you are obliged." Children are brought up to believe that it is an integral part of the Christian creed that the world was made in six days, for instance; and when they have found out that science says differently, they are prepared to find that the rest of their religious teaching has been equally short of the truth. The clergy gain a reputation for disingenuousness and insincerity and fear of truth, and the power of Christianity is hopelessly undermined.

Even at theological colleges the teaching is often neither candid nor practical. There are lectures on "bowdlerized" higher criticism, on "how to get round the thirty-nine articles," "how to explain away the Athanasian creed," and so on. Hours are devoted to proving that chasubles were or were not used in the Elizabethan Church. A bowing acquaintance with the early fathers and the councils is established. Hints are given on visiting, and on intoning the service so as to deprive it of any appearance of sincerity. By means of innumerable "hour" services, the student is schooled to endure with apparent good grace services which have little meaning for him. But very little idea is given of the great truths by which the Christian ought to live, of the things that he ought to desire, and the things that he ought to despise or to fear, of the point of view from which he ought to regard life—in short, of the real Christianity. Perhaps, layman reader, you have no opportunity of knowing whether these charges are justified or not. But is not the dead formalism of so many of our services, and the poverty of so many of our sermons a proof that they are justified?

However, it is time that we went on to make some definite proposals. The first is that the gospels and the apostles' creed should be substituted for the ten commandments as the basis of Christian morality. We have already, in the first part of this book, tried to deal in this way with the gospels. Let us therefore now approach the "Apostles' Creed," looking to it, not for an expression of abstract philosophy, but for a statement of the truths by which we are to be enabled to live a new life.

"I believe in God the Father Almighty, Maker of Heaven and Earth." What is the practical meaning of such a belief? To begin with, if we do not believe in God, we cannot logically believe in our own power to influence our own lives. If there is no God, there is no intelligence or purpose in nature. If there is none in nature, there can be none in us men, who are children of nature. We shall have to say, like a popular critic of religion, "There is, I grant, every appearance of freewill; but it belongs to the category of appearances which deceive." So belief or disbelief in God means all the difference between believing that we can influence our destinies, and believing that we are mere puppets of heredity and circumstance, the helpless spectators of our lives. The vaguest belief in God, therefore, even if we know nothing about Him, is a matter of the utmost importance when properly understood; moreover, the average man, without any learning at all, can come to a conclusion as to whether it is best to believe or to disbelieve in God, simply by trying whether it produces better results to believe in his own will and reason, or to be a cynical spectator of his life.

But, as we have tried to show in the first part of this book, if God is regarded as "the Father Almighty, Maker of Heaven and Earth," the practical effect of belief is greater still. If God is the Father, if He loves us and wishes us well, if He is good, if He is the Almighty Creator, then it means that we must try to love and understand and trust Him. It means that we must try to make Him a recognized factor in our environment, and that in proportion as we succeed, He will predominate over all other influences, and make us free. It means that we must trust our best instincts, believe in our power to become the best that we can imagine, believe in our power to subordinate all our faculties to the attainment of the highest ideals. Moreover, if God is the Father, men are brothers, and it is in loving and loyal co-operation, and not in selfish isolation, that we shall realize the best that is in us. So this "Apostles' Creed" starts off with the very central doctrine of Christianity, from which all others are derived—a doctrine which makes a vital difference to our whole outlook on life, our self-knowledge, our relations with other men. It can be tested, therefore, by experiment. Does it work out in practice to take this view of ourselves, our fellows, and our life? If so, we have established a probability that the first article of the creed is true.

"And in Jesus Christ His only Son, Our Lord." We have seen that unless we can believe in God, we cannot logically believe in ourselves—in the reality of our will and reason and conscience, the spiritual part of us. We might have put it the other way round, and said that it is because as practical men we are obliged to believe in our own spirit that we are obliged to believe in God. It is in the spirit of a man

CATHOLIC TEACHING

that we have the surest evidence for the existence of God. So also it is in the most spiritual human life, which means the freest human life, that we see most of God. If Jesus was, as we have argued, the perfectly free man, He was the fullest revelation of God to men, the only true Son of God. If we believe this, we shall try to imitate Him, to frame our lives on the same principles as He did, to share His point of view. And it is when, in trying to attain to His freedom and courage and love and humility and purity, we find ourselves becoming more truly happy and useful, that we feel that we are proving this second article of the creed.

"Who was conceived by the Holy Ghost, born of the Virgin Mary." As we have already pointed out in Part I, Appendix I, this article of the creed is secondary. It will not in itself make any difference to us whether we believe it or not. If it is necessary, it is necessary as a safeguard of the preceding article.

"Was crucified, dead, and buried." This article is not one that needs defending. No one that matters doubts it. But it is very important. As we pointed out in Part I, it was the death of Jesus which was the supreme test of the reality of His faith. It is the fact that He took into account the injustice and suffering of life, and Himself endured it, that makes it possible for us to believe that His faith was something more than the dream of a poet.

"He descended into Hell." Well, the writer of the creed presumably thought that the world was flat, and that underneath it was a dim chamber where the souls of the dead were immured until the day of judgment. As he knew that a day elapsed between the death of Jesus and His first appearance to the disciples, he concluded that He had descended into that chamber. We do not agree with him in detail; but on the main point, that the same thing happened to Jesus as happens to other men, we are agreed. It is comforting to those who must die to know that their Lord went before them.

"The third day he rose again from the dead. He ascended into heaven." If Jesus rose, and is alive now, we know that He was right to trust death, and that His faith was justified. We also know that He will help us to follow Him. If by praying in His name, and by praying to Him, and by thinking of Him as the living Lord, and by trying to embody Him, we find that we gain strength and contentment and usefulness, we shall have proved that Jesus rose from the dead, and is alive for evermore. If He is simply a dead man, it will not work to suppose that He is alive.

"From thence he shall come to judge the quick and the dead." The writer of this article evidently meant to imply that the world would come to an end while men were still alive on it. This belief is doubtful, and of no real importance. The important thing is to realize that death, which may come at any time, is a call to judgment; and that whereas a good use of "talents" in this life will mean enlarged opportunities and responsibilities hereafter, their misuse will mean deprivation. It will make a big difference to a man if he believes that when he dies he will have to face Jesus, and that Jesus will say to him, either "I was sick, and thou didst visit me . . . " or "I was sick, and thou visitedst me not . . . " and "Inasmuch as thou hast done it unto one of the least of these my brethren, thou hast done it unto me." —See Matthew xxv.

"I believe in the Holy Ghost." If there were no

help to be obtained from God, if there were no Holy Spirit to help our human spirits, it would be in vain for us to try to attain to the Christ ideal of life. We can only conquer the powerful forces within and without us, which try to enslave us, by the aid of a greater force than they. If by faith we become new men, we witness to the Holy Ghost.

" The Holy Catholic Church. The Communion of Saints." It is because we believe that in Christ all who love Him are one, and that in imitating Him each will find his proper place and the proper use of his faculties in the common body, that it is practically possible for us to co-operate lovingly and loyally with other men. In isolation a man is so insignificant that he cannot take himself seriously.

" The forgiveness of sins." This is one of the main results of belief in the fatherhood of God. It is this that makes it possible for us to get up and try again after we have fallen. It is this that makes it possible to pray to God for help. And we know that the forgiveness of sins is true if, when we have really hated our sin, and confessed it, we are enabled to conquer it.

" The resurrection of the body, and the life everlasting." If death is the end, and there is no future life, we shall naturally set our affections on the treasures and sweets of this world. If we believe that death is not the end, we shall try to get the treasure that seems likely to be eternal—purity, love, humility, faith, and so on. If we believe in death we shall esteem men for what they possess ; but if we believe in life we shall esteem them for what they are. To some extent the fact that it is character rather than possessions that produces what we feel to be the best sort of life, is in itself an argument for believing in eternal life. It works best to believe.

But as for the resurrection of the body, I am not at all sure that I understand exactly what it means. If it means the resurrection of the " natural body " to a material life, I claim the precedent of St. Paul for my scepism. If it simply means the survival of personality, I agree.

In the main, then, the " Apostles' Creed " is a good simple statement of the foundation doctrines of Christianity, when it is considered in a practical way. It could evidently be made a useful peg on which to hang Christian instruction. But it is also evident, if what we have said is correct, that it must be used as a help to men, and not as a pistol to be held at their heads. In view of the fact that Christianity is at least a hundred years older than this " ancient baptismal creed of the Roman Church," it must not be regarded as a fetish.

The Bible.

Our second practical suggestion is the issue of a shortened Bible for the use of simple people. We are in very great danger of making the Bible of no effect through our tradition. As a rule we either teach it in such a way as to give the impression that we think it verbally inspired, while keeping open a loophole of escape if we are pressed ; or we teach the higher criticism with such zest that we forget that the books have any religious value. The former way breeds suspicion, and sows the seed of scepticism; the latter wastes the precious hours allotted to religious instruction in an intellectual exercise. The higher criticism is an intensely interesting study, and the picture of the religious history of the Jewish race that it leaves us with is so unique as to be almost a proof of the rule of providence in history. But it is not essential Christianity. It is an extra, though well worth the trouble to those who can give the time to its study.

For the ordinary man and child the value of the Bible lies in the extraordinarily profound sayings and stories with which it abounds, on the supremely important subject of how to live the life that God wants us to live. If a man, as he reads his Bible, habitually underlines any sentence that strikes him as being helpful to think of, his Bible will be heavily scored indeed, and it will be to him a treasure house of endless comfort and inspiration. But there are thousands of verses in the Bible which are of no conceivable value for the ordinary man; and for many the Bible is a closed book, simply because it is so big that they despair of finding their way about it. The experience of a boy on an emigrant ship is probably not unusual. When he left England, full of good intentions, his vicar placed a Bible in his hands, with some such words as, "If you read that every day, my lad, and mark what you read, you will never go far wrong." The boy began at the beginning, intending to read straight through to the end. Somewhere about the middle of Exodus he began to be very considerably bored, finding very little that was of much use to him; so he turned to the end, to the Revelation. This mystified him still more, so he put the book carefully away, with a mental note that though it was doubtless very wonderful, it was rather beyond him. Soon after, he heard it scoffed at by some shallow sceptic, and then even his respect for it ceased, and it was lost. The Bible contains the finest religious literature in the world; but in its present form it is not adapted for the use to which it is put,—as every Christian's manual of life. It is meant to be a help, but we often make it a burden and a stumbling block.

The teaching of children.

In teaching children, surely the important thing is to begin by teaching them what to admire and what to despise, to trust God and to love Jesus. For this purpose some of the Old Testament stories can hardly be bettered; for instance, the stories of Joseph, of the sacrifice of Isaac, of the call of Samuel, of the anointing of David, of David and Goliath, of Daniel in the lions' den, and the three children in the furnace. It does not really matter whether these stories are true or not. They teach a right point of view. They can be mixed up with other legends, such as St. Martin's cloak, St. Christopher, and so on. But with regard to the gospels it does seem important to teach only what one is most sure about. It is surely better to teach the story of the good Samaritan, than that of the wedding at Cana; that of the prodigal son, than that of the Magi. It is so easy to let children fall into the way of regarding the gospel story in the same light as what they will afterwards recognize as fairy stories. It is dangerous to run this risk. They ought to be made to feel from the start that Jesus is real, and different; and that can only be done by avoiding too much emphasis on the miraculous side of the narrative, and concentrating on the divine beauty of the human side.

Conclusion.

The conclusion is that it is of vital importance for the Church to realize that the end to which all teaching should be directed is a horizon widened so as to include God, which will lead on to a new birth into a new life—the Christ-life. Nothing must be taught for its own sake ; but all teaching made to contribute to the end in view.

CHAPTER VII

Catholic Warfare

In the English Church we are very fond of military hymns. We like singing about going into battle, and girding on bright armour. But in our hymns there is amazingly little about our foes. They are described in general terms as " hell " and " hosts of Midian," but seldom, if ever, in language which they might resent as personal.

As a matter of fact an examination of the Church of England leads us to suspect that its ideas as to what it is fighting against are pretty vague. It would certainly be difficult to identify its foes by their wounds. The same could not be said of Jesus Christ. He knew exactly what He was fighting. He was fighting meanness and cant, callousness and cruelty, coarseness and lust, tradition and convention, riches and class pride, physical and moral cowardice ; and the legions of these false gods knew very well that they were being fought, and that is why they patched up their own little quarrels so as to get Him crucified.

These foes of the Master ought to be our foes too ; but in England we hardly seem to realize it. They are very strong. Meanness and cant abound even in the Church, callousness and cruelty are part of the industrial system under which we live, coarseness and lust are everywhere rampant, tradition and convention are the masters of most of our ecclesiastics, riches and class pride are the foundations of modern society and enslave every class, physical and moral cowardice are on the increase, and the latter presides over convocation itself.

These foes really fight in two armies. One army includes callousness, cruelty, coarseness, and lust; and the rest are included in the other. The two armies approach from opposite directions, and their methods of warfare are slightly different; but they work in close combination. It will, however, be convenient to consider them separately.

First we must ask what the Church is doing and what it ought to be doing against callousness and cruelty, coarseness and lust. In the "slums" of our great cities people live in overcrowded and verminous houses. The wages of the men, though earned by long hours of work, are so small, and so irregular, that very often their wives have to work too. This means that homes are left dirty, children neglected, elder children are driven into premature marriage so as to escape from an intolerable home; thrift, self-respect, cleanliness and health are impossible. There is no place of recreation after the long hours of work except the public-house, which entails the ten-fold aggravation of all the evils that we have mentioned. This system is recognized by the Church as an enemy. The Church tries to alleviate its rigours. It encourages education, distributes alms, organizes clubs and places of wholesome amusement. In so doing it is fighting the battle of the Lord. The strength and conviction with which we are fighting this battle have increased enormously in the last few years. And yet we are very far from being whole-hearted and honest in our efforts. The Church is in the main identified with the richer classes. Even in poor parishes it is the less poor who are members of the congregation. Consequently the Church as a whole is only willing to battle up to a point. We are willing to do things for the poor; but we are not willing, we are shocked and grieved, when the poor try to do something for themselves. As soon as labour begins to organize itself our sympathies are alienated. As soon as the government of the country demands in the form of taxes, and the boroughs in the form of rates, the aid that we acknowledge ought to be given, we are up in arms. We will not admit the right of the labourer to freedom and opportunity and self-respect, though we are willing to give him instalments by way of charity.

This is a weakness and disloyalty in the Church, that it fails to recognize that the movement of organized labour to secure the opportunity for good life to all men and women is an ally in the battle against callousness and cruelty, coarseness and lust. We may legitimately think that our ally is not always wise; but we ought at least to appreciate the fact that it is an ally, and that in intention it is on the side of the angels.

The reason why the Church as a whole is not free to take this point of view is that it has made a compact with the other army of Hell, the army of meanness and cant, of tradition and convention, of riches and class-pride, of physical and moral cowardice. The Church as a whole is interested in the preservation of class distinctions, of the rights of property, of traditions and conventions. This fact leads it into a position of meanness and cant from which we have not the courage to break away. The Church is an owner of property; the Church relies on respect for tradition and convention; the bishops

CATHOLIC WARFARE 147

of the Church are peers, its clergy are "gentlemen," its churchwardens are men of property. The Church is not free itself; and therefore it cannot free others, From every poor parish comes the same complaint. "We can fill our clubs, but not our churches; we can distribute blankets but not salvation."

To a great extent the preceding chapters indicate ways in which this intolerable state of affairs might be relieved. If the services and teaching of the Church were made more simple and practical, it might cease to be ruled by the upper classes. If it ceased to fight against the apostles of scientific and historical truth—and they, too, ought to be allies of the Church of Christ—it might be less dependent on tradition and prestige. But more needs to be done. The Church must cease to be identified with one particular class before it can be really free to fight. The Church must declare war on the domination of riches and social pride before it can drive the traitors from its own ranks. How this is to be done deserves very serious consideration.

Rightly or wrongly the Church of England is largely identified with its clergy. When people want to know for what the Church stands they look to the lives of the clergy. They find that the clergy have a fixed position in the social scale. They belong to a particular class. Consequently, the Church is in the mind of the ordinary man identified with that class. A clergyman is expected to beg from the rich, to solicit the patronage of the noble, to mix on terms of equality with the gentry, to condescend to the shopkeepers, and to bully the labourer. He is expected to marry a lady, to live in a gentleman's house, eat a gentleman's food, send his children to a gentleman's school, and to wear a gentleman's clothes. But this is perfectly absurd when one considers that the Founder of his Church was a carpenter, its apostles fishermen; and that he is the prophet and priest of the God before whose throne all human distinctions vanish, the messenger of a kingdom in which servants are princes, and the humble exalted.

The remedy is not easy to see. If a man marries it is inevitable that he should be a member of a class; and we cannot contemplate a celibate clergy, for that means an immoral clergy or an inhuman clergy. And it will be urged that in nearly all cases where men of humble origin have been ordained they have proved even more snobbish than the gentry. Nevertheless we are convinced that it is only by having clergy of all classes that the Church can escape from identification with a particular class.

The reason why the ordination of working men or commercial men has hitherto been a failure surely is simply that on ordination they are expected to ape gentility. As soon as a man is ordained he is expected to wear a gentleman's clothes, etc., etc. But if men who were ordained remained in their own class, they would not be a failure. There is no real reason why there should not be clergy living on thirty shillings a week, sending their children to board schools, and letting them earn their living at shops and factories. It is only because the Church is artificial, because its teaching needs an education in sophistry, and its services require a knowledge of dead languages, and because we have a rooted conviction that class distinctions are of real importance, that we cannot bear to contemplate a clergyman on a "living wage." There is no real reason why the servant of the servants of Christ should be better paid, and live at a higher standard than the brethren whom he serves.

If there is a real reason why all the ministers of the Church of England should be gentlemen, so much the worse for the Church of England, and the sooner it is altered the better.

Money is a real enemy, and yet the lack of it is as great a one. Class pride is inconsistent with Christianity, and yet each class has particular virtues which it holds in trust for the nation. We need " franciscans " to show us the weakness of money and pride, to hold them up to contempt; and yet we cannot all be franciscans. Humility and love can make riches and rank good servants. It is only when the pride of them makes prisoners of humility and love that they are enemies. It is only in so far as riches and rank, or the desire for them, dominate a man and shut him off from the love of God and the fellowship of the Church that they are bad. It is better to renounce all worldly goods than to miss the treasure of eternity; but in renunciation for its own sake there is no virtue. The man who merely renounces the world without gaining the kingdom of Heaven is poorer than he was before. The gospel is not a gospel of poverty, but a gospel of freedom; and poverty is only required when riches and social position mean the imprisonment of the spirit. A better way than renunciation would be, perhaps, to make riches and rank serve the Lord of life; but this is beyond the power of most men. Certainly in the English Church the spirit is not free, and wealth and snobbishness are among our most potent foes.

When the Church of England has broken its compact with the enemies of freedom, and ceased to fight against the friends of justice and truth, and when it is no longer the property of a class, but of all classes, then, and then only, will the kingdom begin to come with power.

CHAPTER VIII

CATHOLIC WARFARE (*continued*)

WE must not leave the subject of Catholic warfare without a reference to certain enemies of the kingdom which, in certain circles, it is the fashion to cry out against. One of these is violence.

Violence shows itself in war, in strikes, in crime, and in the penal system. Against all these, any book which sets out to be up to date must record its vote. And yet it may be argued that perhaps the present Liberal agitation against violence is not quite so certainly and wholly Christian as is often assumed.

Some people may suspect, and not without reason, that there is a little cant about the agitation against war. War is costly, and those who decry it are often lovers of money. War means the momentary dominance of the military character, which is swift and direct in action, simple in motive, ruthless as to results; and those who decry war are sometimes men who wax gross in peace by means not always straight, but have to take a back seat in time of war. War means the shedding of blood, it means hurt and death; and many of those who decry it are men who fear to be reminded of naked realities, and like to live in an artificial atmosphere from which ugly facts are excluded.

War is an evil. It lets loose the primitive passions. It entails suffering and maiming. It leaves a legacy of widows and orphans. When it is waged, as it often has been, in the interests of kings and nobles and capitalists, and at the expense of the people, it is a barbarous and inexcusable thing. But there are things which are worth dying for, as Jesus taught. When small nations that are crushed and oppressed by their powerful neighbours fight for the freedom to live and develop and to make their contribution to history, that is glorious war. Such were the wars for the liberation of Italy and Greece, and to some extent the war between Turkey and the Balkan States. As a matter of fact most of the wars of the last century or two have been waged for freedom. The French revolution, and the earlier wars of Napoleon, the American civil war, the Russo-Japanese war, the Cuban war—all these were at bottom protests on the part of, or on behalf of one nation or part of a nation, against the encroachments of another on its liberty.

We do not want to defend war in principle. We would only utter a warning that before we wax self-righteous on the subject, we should be quite certain of the purity of our motives. There are things which it is a duty to be ready to die for.

Jesus, as a matter of fact, did not value human life so very highly. He was constantly urging His disciples not to overvalue it. And it seems possible that to a certain extent the present horror of war is due to the decay of belief in a future life, and the consequent exaggerated respect for the sanctity of human life. In the eyes of the modern, death is always a tragedy. In the eyes of Jesus it was never a tragedy unless the dead man had lived a contemptible life.

Moreover there is a certain directness and sternness about the military character which is singularly Christlike. Whereas it is by no means certain that the results of peace are pleasing to God at all. In time of peace, meanness and cant and lying and distortion of truth and cringing and unscrupulousness often bring men to the head of affairs. It is a bad thing to kill a man ; but it is a worse thing to cheat him, and to lie to him, and entangle him, and ruin him body and soul. There are worse things than war.

The same meanness and contemptible shrinking from things that hurt is noticcable in the popular attitude towards strikes. In time of strikes the people as a whole have no interest in the rights and wrongs of the quarrel. Their sole preoccupation is to get it settled before it begins to hurt. They do not desire justice but peace. That sort of desire for peace is despicable, and most unchristian. Did not Jesus say " I come to bring, not peace, but a sword ? "

It seems fairly certain that Jesus disliked a hypocritical Pharisee a good deal worse than a bandit. There will be at least one bandit in the Kingdom of Heaven, and we do not know of any hypocrite who was encouraged to hope for admittance. Yet the Church is very horrified at crimes of violence, and only conventionally shocked when it is found that a churchwarden is a slave-driver for six days out of seven.

It is often said that the penal system in general, and capital punishment in particular, are unchristian. Jesus Christ did not believe in punishment for its own sake. One idea of punishment is that it is a payment due to an abstract justice, or to the God of justice. If a man has done so much wrong he must endure so much punishment, so that " justice may be vindicated." This theory Jesus did not believe in, because He knew that God was love before He was justice. Therefore He did not allow the woman taken in adultery to be stoned, because He saw that there was a better way of dealing with her. It would give God no satisfaction to see her stoned, and it would do her no good. On the other hand, clemency might do her good.

At the same time there is another side to punishment. A decent sort of man, who has done a mean thing, generally has a sort of feeling that it would do him a power of good to be hurt. He wants to be kicked, as a sort of sign that he is forgiven, and that the mean thing is forgotten. One would guess from one's own feelings that if a decent sort of man had committed a crime, and was thoroughly ashamed of it, he would much rather be soundly flogged and allowed to go, than be shut up for weeks in a cold and soulless prison. There is a refinement of cruelty which is positively inhuman in the so-called "humanitarianism" of the prison. A prison is merely sordid and callous. It encourages the prisoner to nurse vengeance against society. It is probably infinitely more cruel and pernicious than the summary justice of the oriental despot's whip.

That there is an expiatory value in suffering hurt, however, and that Jesus believed in it, seems to be proved by the fact that He undoubtedly thought that His death would be an atonement for sin. Indeed, as will appear in the next chapter, there is always this element of expiatory suffering in the forgiveness of the Christian sinner. Whether, however, the principle can be applied to the convicted criminal by a society so notoriously hypocritical as ours, is very doubtful. If only they may punish who are without sin, as Jesus seems to say, it would appear as if most criminals ought to be allowed to go free!

The purpose of these remarks may appear rather

obscure. It is, however, quite definite. It is a protest against the idea that any sentimental twaddle is to be accepted as "Christian" simply because it happens to be sentimental.

Marriage and divorce.

Another foe that the Church is very active in fighting is the idea of marriage which does not exclude divorce. In this battle the Church does not seem to have used the right weapons. There has been too much argument about the exact words of our Lord, which are by no means certain, and not enough attempt to understand the point of view from which He regarded the subject.

A good many people look upon marriage simply as a means of gratifying the instinct of sex without running the risks of promiscuous intercourse, and at the same time of fixing the responsibility for the care of the children which may result. Jesus is quite clear that the mere gratification of an animal instinct is a bad thing. Speaking of the commandment "Thou shalt not commit adultery," He said that a man who "lusteth after a woman" has committed adultery with her already in his heart. He also said that it was the pure in heart that should "see God." That is to say, the mere gratification of an animal instinct degrades a man to the level of a beast, and deprives him of the greatest privilege of man—the power to come into touch with God. Marriage was, in the eyes of Jesus, a much more solemn thing than that. Two people, when they marry, enter a union so close that "they are no more two, but one flesh." They are partners with each other and with God in the creation of a child of God. This is what distinguishes the union of men and women from that of animals.

Animals only beget animals. They beget beings which are guided by instinct, and therefore it is quite right that their sexual union should be a matter of instinct. But men and women beget beings that are not only animal, but also rational and emotional and spiritual. Therefore their union carries with it a far greater responsibility. They are partners with God in His greatest work of creation. In their partnership God is a third, and therefore it should not be broken. It is a partnership that God has blessed, and used for His loving purpose of creating children for Himself as well as for them. This is the ideal which must be maintained if marriage is to be anything like what God intended it to be. Nevertheless, " this saying is not for all." In the past, God permitted divorce because of " the hardness of men's hearts " ; and if men's hearts are still hard, and they do not share Christ's point of view, presumably divorce is still to be endured.

The duty of the Church in this matter is to try to make men and women understand and share the point of view of Jesus, and to regard marriage as a holy partnership which ought never to be broken. The question remains, what is the best way of carrying out this duty ? The answer ordinarily given is to try and force on all members of the nation the state of affairs which should result from a right point of view. This seems like putting the cart before the horse. Surely it is quite absurd to suppose that anyone will ever be forced by penalties into taking a point of view which does not commend itself to them. To make a law of the land that which does not correspond to the feelings and convictions of the citizens, is madness. The law ought to embody the average morality of the community. The Church ought not to attempt to interfere with the conditions of civil marriage. On the other hand, if people are married in a church, they ought to be made to understand that they are entering upon an entirely different compact to the civil compact into which they enter at a registry office. They are pledging themselves to an idea of marriage which is not the idea of the community as a whole, but of the Church as the body of Christ. The best way of making this clear would be by making marriage at a registry office compulsory, and making the service in church definitely an extra, corresponding to the extra solemnity which Christ's point of view puts on marriage.

There is still another question, and that is whether divorce ought to be possible to Christians in the case of infidelity. On this point the words ascribed to Jesus are conflicting. In one passage He is represented as permitting divorce in these circumstances, and in another nothing is said of this qualification. Under these circumstances it is difficult to be dogmatic; but one cannot help feeling that unrepentant infidelity makes the continuance of the ideal impossible, and automatically destroys the holiness of the compact. In any case it is not much good enforcing the terms of such a compact on people who have lost the feeling that it is sacred. It is certainly arguable that as marriage is much older than Christianity there should be no compact in Church, but only an explanation of Christ's ideal, and prayer for grace to be able to follow it. After all, marriage, such that divorce is impossible, is only one out of many high ideals which Jesus set before those who desired to enter the kingdom, and it is not quite clear why this alone should be singled out for the application of rigid inquisition and stern penalties. There are many other ways in which men can degrade themselves to the level of beasts, and cut themselves off from God, and if all were punished by ostracism and excommunication and exclusion from the Church, it is to be feared that the Church would become very small indeed. No doubt failure to live up to the ideal is more open and notorious in the case of marriage than in the case of other things; but that is not necessarily a reason why it should be more heavily punished. Also, if the rule against divorce were to be rigidly enforced, the married lives which would result might be conventionally respectable; but they certainly would not be holy. It may be that unhappy marriages should be left, like other failures, to the reproach of the "still small voice" of conscience, and that the Church should confine itself to making certain that the voice is heard.

CHAPTER IX

THE WAY OF SALVATION

ONE of the central doctrines of Christianity is that the death of Jesus upon the Cross saves us from sin, and yet it is a doctrine which the Church is very much at a loss to explain. Reams have been written about it, and still the plain man repeats with a puzzled air, "I don't see how it can." Yet if it is to do the work of Jesus, the Church must understand the way of salvation.

Supposing that a man is the slave of a really bad vice, a vice that is mean in itself, and which affects other people besides himself. Suppose, for instance, that he is the victim of the drug habit, and while a slave to it leads a young fellow into the same vice. Suppose that in time he comes to realize the full beastliness of his sin, and is able to give it up; but that the youth whom he has led astray has got beyond his control, and goes on being ruined by that vice. Imagine that man going to God for forgiveness, and in utter shame confessing what he has done. Imagine him receiving from the priest the assurance that he is really forgiven if he really repents. Is this the end? Does he henceforth have an easy conscience? Does he feel that his sin is as if it never was? Will he feel qualified to go about with a bright and innocent look in his eyes, asking others, "Are you saved"?

On the contrary, he knows that his sin is not wiped out, for he sees the effect of it still on the youth whom he led astray. Not all his tears or fastings or prayers can undo what he has done, or give him peace.

If he is at rest in his mind, and goes about prating of his salvation, the youth whom he has wronged will with some justice mock him as a hypocrite.

Such a man will know no peace until he is assured that the youth who suffers for what he has done will in the end be restored to sanity. This assurance the Christian doctrine of the atonement gives him. In the person of the Son, God Himself has taken upon Him the burden of our sins, with His stripes we are healed. This simply means that the cross was the sign and the proof to us of the absolutely infinite love of God for us—love which has no limits, and will even suffer for us that we may live.·

We know from everyday experience that the suffering of the innocent for the guilty has great power. It is the love of innocent and pure women, for instance, which can alone undo the wrong that men do to those whom they seduce. It is the loving care of the hospital doctors and nurses that undoes the harm done by the employer of sweated labour, who rakes in his shekels at the cost of the health and lives of men and women. All through life, men and women are bearing each other's burdens, and atoning for each other's sins. And the power to bear the burden that another has laid is proportionate to one's own innocence and love. And now into this process comes infinite love and infinite innocence, the love and innocence of the Son of God. Hence we know that in the end all the evil of the world will work itself out on Him, and will be expiated.

Even so, our sinner will not be satisfied. He will not be content to watch and see His Lord suffering for him. His prayer, if he is really repentant, will be, "Lord, give me something to do, give me some burden to bear, that I too may love." This is the instinct of the wholesome man, and Jesus Christ does not deny his request. His answer is, "Be a member of my body; share my suffering for the sins of the world; be crucified with me." And the man will be glad that he is accounted worthy to suffer in the name of the Lord Jesus.

So, and only so, is the Christian salvation perfect. It gives not only forgiveness and peace, but the self-respect which only comes from work. The Church is the body of Christ, and it is only a living body if its members suffer with Him for the sins of the world, and in love and humility try to help others to bear their burdens.

CHAPTER X

Conclusion

WHEN all beauty and all simplicity are found in worship; when all vain traditions and sophistries have been done away with; when its teaching is clear and practical and simple, and proved by its results; when it fights all its foes and recognizes all its allies; when it includes all classes; when it has a way of salvation for all sinners; when love and humility abound,—then the Church will be the Catholic Church, the body of Christ.

The day will come, perhaps sooner than we think, when the storms will beat again against the Church, and will wash away much that has been built on a foundation of sand. In those days the Church will be left poor and diminished and without social influence. Yet in those days perhaps it will have more freedom, more sincerity, more faith, more love, more courage ; and then many will see the Spirit of the divine Carpenter in the body of His Church who look in vain as yet.

Meanwhile, however diseased the body that we offer to Christ may be, in it the blood still circulates, and the heart still beats ; and if any member really wants to be a living member, and is really willing to remove the obstructions that hinder his health, Jesus will give him the life and vigour that is eternal.

APPENDIX I

The Virgin Birth and the Empty Tomb

It is not the object of this book to pronounce judgment on questions which are being disputed among Churchmen; but it is impossible wholly to ignore them. Without being dogmatic, we would wish to help the ordinary Churchman in a practical manner.

Those who make it their business to attack Christianity are fond of pointing out that the virgin birth and the resurrection of the body are stories which cannot be historically proved true; and they think that in so doing they are undermining the foundations of Christianity. It is important to realize that they are mistaken. These stories cannot be proved true simply because they are miraculous, and no ancient evidence can be accepted as decisive when the event referred to is in itself improbable. If the historian were to accept the miracles of the gospels simply on the evidence of the evangelists, he would be obliged, in order to be consistent, to accept equally those recorded of, say, Apollonius. It is only the fact that the virgin birth and the bodily resurrection are told of Jesus that makes them appear credible to those who believe in Jesus. In other words, none can be asked to believe that Jesus was the Son of God because He is said to have been born of a virgin, and to have risen bodily from the grave; though it may happen that a person who believes, on other grounds, that Jesus was the Son of God, and is now alive, may feel that the stories of the virgin birth and the resurrection of the body are for that reason either probably, or even necessarily true. To them the story told by St. Luke will be acceptable. That is to say that though these stories are not evidence of the divine sonship of Jesus, they may be regarded as implied by it. Since, however, the divine sonship of Jesus cannot be proved by these stories, it follows that it cannot be disproved by their rejection. It must also be pointed out that the rejection of these stories does not necessarily discredit the remainder of the gospels of which they are a part, because all higher critics are agreed that they are derived from different sources to the rest of the gospels.

This much may be regarded as historically proved:

(1) That in the Jewish, that is to say the earliest, stage of Christianity, it was believed that Jesus was virgin-born.

(2) That the earliest disciples were absolutely convinced that Jesus was risen from the dead, and alive and present with them. It was their conviction on this point that gave them the faith and power to preach after the crucifixion.

(3) That the body of Jesus was neither produced by His enemies to disprove the resurrection, nor preserved for superstitious veneration by the disciples.

The man who has recognized the freedom of Jesus, and has found freedom and power in trying to imitate Him and to share His point of view, and by praying in His name to His Father, and who has found love and fellowship and life as a member of His body the Church, will not easily doubt either that He was the Son of God, or that He is alive. The man who has not experienced any of these things, nor recognized them in others, has not understood the foundations of Christianity.

APPENDIX II

The Miracles of Jesus

THERE are some people who simply cannot believe the miracles of the gospels, and there are others who apparently cannot see the difficulty of believing them. The present note is intended primarily for those who cannot believe.

First of all let us define exactly what we mean by the miracles. Presumably we do not deny that Jesus performed " works of healing," since we know that " psychiatry " is now a recognized faculty, and its limits are not by any means ascertained. In fact we should probably agree that though the " works of healing " may well have been miracles in the eyes of the disciples of Jesus, they would not so appear to us. As a matter of fact it is rather doubtful whether at the time they were considered so very very wonderful. They seem to have differed only in degree from cures performed by other men. They were sufficient to call forth delight and astonishment, love and reverence, but they were not " signs from heaven." People in those days seem to have set a good deal of store by " signs from heaven." The Pharisees demanded one, and probably the disciples ardently desired one. But whenever the matter was mentioned to Jesus He appears to have been distinctly discouraging. The reason was evidently that He had considered the subject carefully during the forty days' fast which preceded His actual ministry, and had come to the conclusion that they were things which no one had a right to demand.

The idea that Jesus discouraged miracle-hunting also receives support from the fact that He always tried to minimize the wonder attaching to His cures.

Often He ascribed the cure to the faith of the patient, at other times to prayer. Often He imposed, or tried to impose, secrecy. In the case of the child raised from the dead He said that she was not really dead.

Similarly when the disciples were most exalted He apparently always started talking about His death, *e.g.*, after the transfiguration.

We must therefore acknowledge the possibility that the disciples, surrounding Jesus with a halo of mystery on account of His healing powers, were on the look out for miracles where there were none, and that they did not as a rule dare to discuss them with Jesus because He was so discouraging, but nursed them all the more in private, and in their talks with each other.

This tendency is not likely to have diminished among the disciples of the disciples, in fact we know from the "apocryphal" gospels that eventually miracle mongering became very common among certain Christians. Indeed it has been said with some justice that the best argument for the gospel miracles is that they compare so favourably with the obvious fabrications of such books as "The Gospel of the Infancy."

Now as a matter of fact the number of "nature miracles" in the synoptic gospels is very small. Excluding the virgin birth, the resurrection, and the miracles of healing, they only number nine :—

1. Walking on the sea.
2. The miraculous draught of fishes.
3. The stilling of the storm.
4. The coin in the fish's mouth.
5. The blasting of the barren fig tree.
6. The feeding of the five thousand.
7. The feeding of the four thousand.

APPENDICES

8. The transfiguration.
9. The voice at the baptism and at the transfiguration.

Of these the majority can very easily be explained away if we want to do so, without casting any suspicion of chicanery on Jesus or of dishonesty on His disciples. The ordinary explanations are as follows: The first three are examples of coincidence into which the wonder-seeking disciples read a miracle without telling Jesus. This is a perfectly feasible explanation of all three. In such cases the memory of details is wonderfully obliging if lacking in accuracy, as every teller and most hearers of good stories, and as many judges and barristers know from their own experience. The fourth is probably a second or third-hand distortion of a story to the effect that Peter was ordered to catch a fish and sell it for a stater. The fifth is quite possibly a version of the parable of the withered fig tree. The sixth and seventh are probably duplicates, and may have been founded on a sort of symbolic meal of Jesus and His disciples, rather after the style of the last supper. The people took small crumbs of bread as a sign of their loyalty to the Master, and perhaps found that their hunger was for the time appeased through their minds being greatly stirred in another direction. The transfiguration may easily have been founded on the sight of Jesus praying in the midst of the glorious hues of dawn during the momentary lifting of an early morning mist. The voice at the baptism was, according to St. Mark, only heard by Jesus Himself, and may have been His picture of a subjective experience.

The question is whether, in accepting, or even in putting forward these possible "explanations" of the miracles of the synoptic gospels, we are taking from or adding to the picture of Jesus our Lord. For ourselves we are bound to confess that we think that we are making the picture more human and no less divine. These " miracles " are not the results of an extension of the powers ordinarily possessed by men. No one ever expects to be able to make five loaves into bread for even five hundred people. It is the sort of thing that we can form no mental picture of, and it does not seem to have any significance except as a " sign " such as our Lord steadily refused to attempt. If anyone finds that the story fits in with his mental picture of Jesus, by all means let him believe it. To him it is credible. We merely claim freedom to doubt that which we cannot endow with any probability or meaning.

NOTE

With regard to the first three miracles in the above list, perhaps we ought to have made our meaning clearer by pointing out that sudden storms do sometimes subside as quickly as they arise, that one may get out of one's course on a foggy night when the wind is contrary, and think that one is further from land than one is, and that it might happen that a school of fish should be seen from the shore though invisible from a boat. Once again we repeat that good stories have a trick of bettering themselves, even when passed on by honest fishermen. The presence of such stories in the gospels is absolutely no argument against their accuracy in other respects.

It may be as well to point out that both the virgin birth and the resurrection stand on quite a different plane. The stories of the virgin birth are undoubtedly derived from other sources than the main bulk of the synoptic gospels, and must therefore be judged separately. The resurrection had such enormous and far-reaching effects that it can only have rested on the most unalterable and well-founded conviction on the part of the disciples.

APPENDIX III

THE RELATIVE VALUE OF THE GOSPELS

ON the whole the ancient tradition that Luke and Mark, the individuals mentioned in the epistles, wrote the third and second gospels, holds the field to-day. Matthew the apostle certainly did not write the first gospel, though he may have contributed to it ; while the authorship of the fourth gospel is still a matter of heated controversy.

In their present form, Mark is the oldest gospel, and is reproduced almost word for word in the first and second. There are traces, however, of a still older gospel in " Matthew " and Luke, a gospel which consisted chiefly of sayings of Jesus. There is also other matter in Matthew and Luke, some of which is ancient and reliable, and some of which is probably legendary. Probably the writings which were used by the compilers of our first three gospels were written between A.D. 40 and A.D. 90, the date of the crucifixion being about A.D. 30. The gospel of St. John is generally thought to be an entirely original document, and not a compilation, though Wendt has an ingenious theory to the contrary. Even if it was written by John, the son of Zebedee, or by the somewhat apocryphal " John the elder, the disciple of the Lord," it was probably not written till about A.D. 95.

We may therefore take as fairly authentic the first three gospels, especially the sayings of Jesus, which are found in Matthew and Luke, and the main narrative in Mark. The legends in Matthew which refer to the birth and crucifixion of Jesus are probably not very reliable. We must also be on our guard in considering some of the sayings of our Lord about the end of the world, specially the long discourse in Mark xiii. and the parallel chapters in Matthew and Luke. The reason is that to begin with it is quite obvious that a long rambling discourse would be very much more difficult to remember than the stories and comments and short pithy sayings in which the teaching of Jesus is generally expressed; and, in the second place, the disciples certainly had their own ideas as to how the kingdom was likely to come, and almost certainly tried to read the confirmation of those ideas into the words of Jesus.

Higher criticism requires little more than common sense, and the man who reads the gospels in an intelligent way will not have much doubt about the teaching or opinions of Jesus, even if he has never read any higher criticism.

The gospel of John is a puzzle. On the one hand it contradicts the synoptists[1], in some respects, in a way which compels us to prefer the latter; while, on the other, the gospel of John can be proved to be right as against the synoptists in matters such as the date of the last supper and the crucifixion. The synoptists give us to understand that Jesus seldom if ever taught who He was; but left people to draw their own conclusions from what He did and taught, and from the way in which He did it. John, on the other hand, represents Jesus as continually enlarging on His exact relations to the Father. In this matter we are bound to doubt John, because the sermons which he puts into the mouth of Jesus are so long and deep that they could not have been remembered for all those years after only being heard once. It is most likely that they represent what John himself

[1] Matthew, Mark, and Luke are called the Synoptists because they take the same point of view.

thought was the right explanation of all that Jesus was and did and said, and that he put it into the mouth of Jesus as a sort of dramatic fiction. At the same time these thoughts of John do seem to be grouped round actual words of Jesus. Such sayings as " I am the good shepherd," " I am the light of the world," " I am the vine," " Labour not for the meat which perisheth," " Except a man be born again he cannot see the kingdom of God," etc., have the same ring about them as the sayings of Jesus in the other gospels.

Again, whereas the synoptists represent Jesus as deliberately refusing to give a sign, or to make capital out of His mighty works, John represents Him as appealing to them as a witness of the truth of His claim to be divine.

It is best to regard the gospel of John as a very good sermon or commentary on the life of Jesus, rather than as a strictly accurate account of that life.

Whether it was written by John the Apostle is uncertain. There is an early tradition that it was. On the other hand, many people feel that it is not the sort of book that a Galilean fisherman would be likely to have written. It is, however, rather unwise to be too dogmatic about what a fisherman might or might not have written if, early in life, he had been a companion of Jesus.